Teaching College Writing
to Diverse Student Populations

Dana R. Ferris

The Michigan Series on Teaching Academic English in U.S. Post-Secondary Programs

Series Editors: Patricia Byrd, Joy M. Reid, and Cynthia M. Schuemann

Ann Arbor
THE UNIVERSITY OF MICHIGAN PRESS

ISBN-13: 978-0-472-03337-9

2012   2011   2010   2009   4   3   2   1

SERIES EDITOR PREFACE

W ELCOME TO *TEACHING COLLEGE WRITING TO DIVERSE STUDENT POPULATIONS*. THE focus of *The Michigan Series on Teaching Academic English in U.S. Post-Secondary Programs* is to explore topical issues relevant to the teaching and learning of English for Academic Purposes (EAP). The series is motivated by our belief that we can do a better job of helping ESL students transition to higher education, meet the challenging academic demands of post-secondary work, and enjoy success as they graduate with two- and four-year degrees. The books in the series are aimed at educators in post-secondary settings who are seeking insights based on both practice and research.

Dana Ferris' book meets every criterion of the series. Her research in L2 writing with international and resident students has been substantial and seminal. In particular, her well-designed and carefully described research with who she calls "early-arriving resident" L2 students has provided teachers with core knowledge of this group's similarities with and especially differences from the more traditionally educated international students. In addition, her student-based research with issues in all ESL writing classes, particularly editing and revision, and her teacher-focused research, especially with response and error feedback, have formed a foundation for more successful ESL learning and teaching.

I (Joy) first met Dana at a TESOL Convention and was amazed both by her youth and her expertise. Good, I thought, she will have years and years of research and teaching to offer the field. Dana has not disappointed: her funded research on ESL writing, her many graduate students who have supported and furthered that research, and her dedication to sharing her results with others have changed the face of ESL writing.

In my early ESL career, I was not surprised to discover that "international students" was an overreaching label that included much diversity. Specifically, the cultural and educational backgrounds of students in an international L2 writing class differed; I was delighted to discover the concept of contrastive rhetoric because it broadened my approaches to teaching. In *Teaching College Writing to Diverse Student Populations*, Dana examines the diversity among L2 resident students, based on what she calls their "educational pathways." Her thoughtful, research-based analysis describes the ways in which these students' "introduction and exposure to English in general and written English in particular, had a huge impact on what they brought into the English language and literacy classroom and how they would respond to various types of instruction." As a result, this book benefits teachers, and thus benefits their students who are transitioning from secondary to post-secondary academic writing.

Teaching College Writing to Diverse Student Populations is filled with specific and practical suggestions for teaching diverse L2 writing students. The information is clear and accessible, and the examples are easy to implement. In other words, Dana offers a terrific resource for teachers and teachers-in-preparation. Enjoy!

Joy M. Reid
Cynthia M. Schuemann
Patricia Byrd

PREFACE

$2$008 MARKED MY 25ᵀᴴ YEAR IN THE TESOL/SECOND LANGUAGE WRITING FIELD, AND I have been a fascinated witness to and participant in a great deal of activity over those years. When I first began my TESOL graduate training in 1983, I found myself immediately tutoring ESL students in the campus writing center. At the time, we talked mainly about "international students" when we discussed ESL issues, even though at this university, the ESL population also included a number of refugees who had fled Iran after the fall of the Shah in 1979, so they were not technically "international" as to their visa status. It was much later that I began to understand that the "who" of second language (L2) instruction was not identical to the "how"—that "L2 writers" were not a homogeneous group. Of course I knew that they had different linguistic and cultural backgrounds, personalities, and learning style preferences, but what I did not realize in the early years was that the students' various educational pathways, especially as to their introduction and exposure to English in general and written English in particular, had a huge impact on what they brought into the English language and literacy classroom and how they would respond to various types of instruction.

As I completed my education and gained additional teaching experience in various parts of California, I became keenly aware that the student landscape had changed dramatically since my first exposure to it. At my first post-doctoral position, the vast majority of students in the ESL program were immigrants, not internationals, and many of them had already been in the United States for a number of years and had completed all or most of their secondary education here. In subsequent years, there has been increased attention from researchers and materials developers in understanding the needs of different L2 student audiences and developing approaches to meeting those needs. Nonetheless, we are still in the early stages of *understanding* today's L2 college/university students, let alone *designing, implementing,* and *assessing* practical changes to better serve them now and in the future.

As noted in the preface to Harklau, Losey, and Siegal's (1999) landmark collection, *Generation 1.5 Meets College Composition,* most of the impact of the so-called "Generation 1.5" student in public schools and colleges has thus far been felt in high-immigration states such as California, Texas, and New York. However, there is both statistical and anecdotal evidence that these demographic patterns are changing (or will be soon); even states with relatively little ethnic or cultural diversity are beginning to notice and ask questions about long-term resident immigrants in their classes (see, for instance, Muchisky & Tangren, 1999). As shifts in student population become more widespread, there is an even greater need for L2 specialists, composition specialists, and program administrators and developers in colleges and universities to understand and adapt to the needs of the changing student audience(s).

This book is designed as an entry-level treatment of the topic of diverse L2 student audiences in U.S. post-secondary education. It is appropriate for those interested in working with students in academic settings, especially those students who are transitioning from secondary to post-secondary education. For L2 professionals who, like me, have gradually become aware of the shift over time, it provides a coherent synthesis and summary not only of the scope and nature of the changes but of their practical implications for program administration, course design, and classroom instruction—in short, a good deal of information we have been aware of in bits and pieces now put in one relatively concise volume. For pre-service teachers and those new(er) to the field of working with L2 students, it offers an accessible and focused look at the "audience" issues with many practical suggestions. For teacher-educators and administrators, it offers a resource that can inform their own decision-making.

I would also add that my own view of the prospective readership for this book has shifted a bit over the past year or two as I have read, thought, and written about various ideas. I no longer see this project as a book solely "for ESL teachers teaching ESL classes," but rather as a more broadly based look at the needs of L2 students in *all* sectors of the college/university context—in ESL/English remedial and college-level reading/writing courses, in general education courses, and in courses in their chosen disciplines. I also have found myself focusing not only on ESL or writing courses but also on various types of support services that can and should be available to L2 students throughout their higher education. As a result, other possible audiences for this book include mainstream (or first language/L1) composition instructors, writing program administrators, and Writing Across the Curriculum (WAC) specialists conducting workshops and providing support for disciplinary faculty.

Because this volume is relatively short and, I hope, reader friendly, it should be a helpful resource for busy instructors and administrators. It could be an excellent addition to a reading list for teacher preparation courses in ESL methods (especially those focusing on academic language and reading/writing skills) and in mainstream composition. With an eye to its potential use for pre-service and in-service training, I have added a few reflection/discussion questions to the end of each chapter.

Focus and Structure

As we consider the characteristics and needs of different language learner audiences in post-secondary education, the discussion will primarily emphasize academic literacy issues—reading and especially writing. In most four-year settings, any "ESL" instruction offered typically involves composition, although some programs offer "reading and composition" courses for L2 students and a few even offer separate "college reading" courses. While academic listening and speaking skills are important (see Ferris, 1998; Ferris & Tagg, 1996a, 1996b; Flowerdew, 1994; Murphy, 2006), the fact is that few four-year institutions offer instruction or assistance with these skills for L2 learners. Thus, most of the history and research in L2 instruction in higher education has emphasized reading and writing skills. While sub-topics related to academic oral skills are certainly discussed in this book (see especially Chapters 2 and 5), the focus is heavily, and intentionally, on **the development of academic reading and writing abilities.**

The book is divided into three sections. Part 1 (Chapters 1–2) provides research-based definitions and descriptions of the various L2 student audiences co-existing in U.S. higher education today, together with an in-depth discussion of the implications of their differing pathways to English for their academic language and literacy development. This first section also introduces three exemplars, John, Hector, and Luciana, who respectively represent the three broad student groups **(international students, late-arriving resident students, early-arriving resident students)** defined in this section. (These are pseudonyms.)

Part 2 (Chapters 3–5) examines the practical implications of understanding the different student groups—first (Chapter 3) at the general level of program administration (with sub-topics such as identification, placement, assessment, and teacher preparation), then moving to more specific emphases on course design (Chapter 4) and classroom instruction (Chapter 5). While Chapters 4 and 5 do not cover the various sub-topics within them in the depth that book-length treatments on teaching L2 reading or writing might, they provide an introductory look at the issues a teacher of L2 students might consider and some practical suggestions that could be applied to a range of teaching situations.

The final part (Chapter 6 and Postscript) attempts to answer the question, "Where do we go from here?" As I have already noted, many L2 and composition professionals are still in the very early stages of understanding the nature and scope of the changes in student audience and have not begun in earnest to consider possible modifications in the ways in which programs, courses, and instruction might be approached. This final section outlines some current models that appear to have promise, makes some suggestions as to guiding principles suggested by the discussion in the previous two sections, and outlines a broad agenda for future research related to the issues raised by the literature and in this book. The Postscript urges both L2 writing and mainstream composition professionals to work collaboratively on serving the students in their particular contexts most effectively.

ACKNOWLEDGMENTS

I am grateful to several groups of people for their assistance with this project. First, I must thank the Research and Creative Activity Subcommittee at California State University, Sacramento (CSUS) (where I was employed at the time of writing) for an assigned-time grant for the 2007–08 academic year, which enabled me to complete the project on schedule. Second, I would like to thank my former students in TESOL preparation courses at CSUS who provided the student background data and text samples for the various individuals profiled in the book; in particular I want to mention Lisa Clark, Cara Tupper, and Ann Michaels, who allowed me to use modified profiles of John, Hector, and Luciana in Chapters 1–2, and Brigitte Rabie, who allowed me to use the student text excerpt shown in Chapter 4.

Third, I thank the professionals from the TESOL Second Language Writing Interest Section listserv who took the time to respond to the informal survey described in Chapter 6. Finally, I am most grateful to the series editors, Pat Byrd, Joy Reid, and Cynthia Schuemann, and our University of Michigan Press editor, Kelly Sippell, and the two reviewers commissioned by Michigan (Sharon Cavusgil of Georgia State University and Paul Kei Matsuda of Arizona State University) for their constructive support during the proposal and writing process.

On a personal level, I must acknowledge my family, especially my husband, Randy Ferris, and my younger daughter, Melissa Ferris, who tolerated some distraction and neglect during the months of writing. My older daughter, Laura Ferris, though now away at college, is always among my biggest supporters and never fails to brighten my day. My love and thanks to all three of you, and you will *occasionally* get some home-cooked meals now . . . until the next project!

Dana Ferris

CONTENTS

PART 1
Foundations

Chapter 1

Defining L2 Student Audiences

The picture that emerges . . . is of a tremendously diverse student population along continua of language proficiency, language affiliation, and academic literacy backgrounds.

—Harklau, Siegal, & Losey, 1999, p. 5

Higher education in the United States is changing rapidly. More students than ever before are attending at least some college—by some estimates, nearly 75 percent of American adults will do so (Wurr, 2004)—and the linguistic, cultural, ethnic, and socioeconomic diversity of the student population is unprecedented (Schwartz, 2004; Shin & Bruno, 2003; U.S. Department of Education, 2003; Wurr, 2004). This volume focuses on the **second language student** in two- and four-year institutions and specifically at how the "second language" (L2) population has shifted over recent decades, evolving into not one but at least three audiences, or groups of students, with distinct characteristics and differing needs. The purpose of this initial chapter is to provide definitions of terms and descriptions of these L2 student audiences (see Figure 1.1)—**international students, late-arriving resident students, and early-arriving resident students**—and to outline practical questions arising from these distinctions that will be addressed throughout the book.

History of Second Language Higher Education: Teaching and Research

Before defining the three student audiences more precisely, we will first consider second language students in higher education from a historical perspective. To begin, some basic definitions are in order. The term *second language students* refers here to "any student whose primary or first language is not English." The term will be used regardless of whether or not the L2 student is also literate in his/her L1 or knows/speaks/writes in additional languages. As we will discuss, in the case of some early-arriving students, it can be difficult even to identify which language is the "first" language, but in most instances it will refer to *the language primarily*

FIGURE 1.1

Basic Terms Used in This Book

Term	Definition
Second language (L2) student*	Students whose first language (the language to which they were exposed in the home as young children) is not English
International student	L2 students born, raised, and educated in another country who come **temporarily** to the U.S. on a foreign student visa for a short-term educational or training program *with the **stated** intent to return to the home country when the program is completed*
Late-arriving resident student	L2 students who intend to reside permanently in the U.S. and who arrived after age 10 and/or who have been in the U.S. fewer than eight years
Early-arriving resident student	L2 resident students who were born in the U.S. to immigrant parents, who arrived in the U.S. prior to age 10, or who have been in the U.S. eight years or longer

*Other terms used: *bilingual, ESL, multilingual* (used synonymously with *L2*), and *Generation 1.5.*

spoken by parents and other adult relatives in the home during the student's early years, prior to beginning school or becoming literate*. It should also be noted that the terms *ESL* and the more recent *multilingual* student appear in the literature, and they will be used at times in this book as synonyms to *L2 students*.

In the brief history of L2 instruction in higher education, most attention has been focused on **international** students (Matsuda, 2006a; Matsuda & Matsuda, 2009). The number of international students in U.S. colleges and universities (including community colleges and pre-university intensive English programs) has increased rapidly since the end of World War II, from a mere 6,570 in 1940 to more than half a million in 2007 (Institute of International Education [IIE], 2007; Matsuda, 2006b; Matsuda, Cox, Jordan, & Ortmeier-Hooper, 2006). As for first- and second-generation immigrants, relatively few attended college: The rate of college attendance in the United States overall was much lower at the beginning of that era than it is now, and immigrant students especially were constrained by economic limitations and family/cultural expectations (see Matsuda, 2003a, for a historical overview).

However, student demographics began to shift in the 1960s following major changes to U.S. immigration law and to admission policies at institutions of higher education, particularly community colleges (Bosher & Rowekamp, 1998; Browning et al., 2000; Harklau, Losey, & Siegal, 1999[1]; McKay & Wong, 2000; Roberge, 2002; Singhal, 2004). As a result, the L2 population at post-secondary institutions increasingly consisted not only of international students but also **resident immigrants,** such as refugees from war-torn Southeast Asian countries and others seeking economic opportunity or religious or political asylum. While some arrived in the United States as adults and sought higher education to learn English and/or for economic advancement, most arrived as children or adolescents with their parents, graduating from U.S. high schools prior to matriculating at colleges or universities.

As noted by Bosher and Rowekamp (1998), the changing student audience in post-secondary ESL classes was not immediately noticed[2] because the first wave of Southeast Asian refugees in the early-to-mid 1970s was relatively affluent and well educated and thus relatively similar to the existing international student population. However, later immigrants had fewer economic and educational advantages, and as their children made their way into college, the differences between these students and the "traditional" ESL population became more apparent. Throughout the 1980s and 1990s, the proportions of bilingual long-term resident immigrants in U.S. higher education increased, and in some states they comprised the vast majority of L2 writers in ESL writing courses (Goen, Porter, Swanson, & vanDommelen, 2002; Harklau, Siegal, & Losey, 1999). More recently, in a 2006 survey of undergraduates in the University of California system, it was found that some 60 percent of the current students are either immigrants themselves or children of first-generation immigrants, and 35 percent reported that English was not their first language (Locke, 2007).[3]

Although secondary and post-secondary ESL teachers (especially in high-immigration areas) have noticed the growing number of resident immigrant students in their classes for the past 20 years or so, serious scholarly attention to the shifting demographics and blurring boundaries really began in the late 1990s with the publication of an edited collection entitled *Generation 1.5 Meets College Composition* (Harklau et al., 1999). Despite the contributions of the Harklau et al. volume, a theme issue of the *CATESOL Journal* (Goen et al., 2002), a theme issue of the online *Reading Matrix* journal (November, 2004), and various other pieces published in journals and books over the past ten years, we are still in the early stages of understanding the characteristics and needs of what McKay and Wong (2000) call "the new immigrant" in college and university writing/language programs. Empirical research on immigrant student writers has been scarce and largely confined to small-scale case studies (Harklau et al., 1999), and with the exception of a study by Bosher and Rowekamp (1998) and a forthcoming study completed in New Zealand by Bitchener (2008), no direct quantitative comparisons between international and immigrant student writers have been attempted.

This brief history of L2 students in U.S. higher education over the past 50 years informally highlights the three L2 student audiences who are the focus of this book: the "traditional" ESL **international** (visa) student, **late-arriving residents,** and **early-arriving residents** (children of first-generation immigrants). As we will see, defining these populations is not as straightforward as it sounds, as there is some dispute among scholars as to where "early arrival" begins and ends, and terms such as *Generation 1.5* are not always used consistently in the literature. Before we turn to these definitions and debates, perhaps a clearer picture of the three audiences can be painted through three stories of real L2 students currently pursuing degrees at state universities in California.

Different Student Audiences: Three Stories

John[4] is a senior business major at a large state university in California. An **international** student from Hong Kong, he has been pursuing his undergraduate degree in the United States for five years. When he was interviewed, he was taking an ESL class in the campus Learning Skills Center to improve his writing so that he could pass the university's Writing Proficiency Examination (WPE), which he had already failed once the previous semester. This class was the lowest-level course in the program, a full two semesters below the first-year composition level. However, it also enrolled upper-division students such as John who needed to improve their skills to meet graduation requirements. Before coming to the United States for college, John had studied English in Hong Kong beginning in the eighth grade. He is well educated and literate and fluent in his first language, Mandarin. He feels that he has a strong grasp on English grammar rules because grammar was the main focus of his EFL classes in Hong Kong. However, he did not have much experience writing in English before entering the United States.

John does not feel confident as a writer in either his L1 or L2, and when asked what he considers his strengths in writing, he said that he did not have any. However, he had a lot to say about his weaknesses. According to John, he has a very hard time putting his thoughts to paper, and writing in English is more difficult because he tries to translate from his L1. He seems frustrated that he does not have a larger vocabulary in English. He wants to use more sophisticated language and sentence structure but is unable to.

A sample of John's writing (shown and discussed in Chapter 2) demonstrates strengths in macro- and micro-level organization and weaknesses in idea development, grammar, and word choice. He has clearly learned some things about inter- and intra-paragraph cohesion (such as the use of transitional phrases to mark relationships among ideas), but his writing still shows many problems in both content and accuracy. Based on this sample, if he does not make rapid and substantial progress, he will pass neither the course he is in nor the WPE. John wonders why at this late stage of his degree program and after so many years of English study he is still in such a low-level ESL class and why he has so many problems with his writing. It is a legitimate question.

Hector, who is 19 years old, is a **late-arriving resident** student from Ensenada, Mexico, and he has been in the United States for two years. He currently attends a state university in southern California and is taking a freshman composition course. (This program, like many others, does not offer separate or designated sections of the first-year course for L2 students.) Although he has been in the United States for a very short time, he began learning English in school in Ensenada when he was six years old. Hector can speak, read, and write both English and Spanish, but it is unclear what his prior experience in writing *academic English* has been. Over the years, he has had a good deal of exposure to English; however, his writing (shown and discussed in Chapter 2) reflects his relatively limited exposure to the English language.

Hector does not enjoy writing in English and only writes what is required for school. A sample text he provided was a summary based on several chapters of *Huckleberry Finn,* which his class was reading at the time. His summary shows that he has good basic comprehension of the plot and conflicts in the novel. However, it does not necessarily show competent academic summary-writing skills, and there are errors in spelling, word choice, sentence boundaries, and punctuation. Though there are strengths in his writing that show good acquisition of written English, if his writing continued at this level, he would most likely not pass freshman English and might have trouble succeeding in other classes.

Luciana is an **early-arriving resident** student and a freshman at a California State University campus. Born in California to Mexican migrant-worker parents, her life and education have been divided seasonally between Mexico and the United States. She is thus what Roberge (2002) described as a *transnational* student. She is enrolled in a basic writing course (one semester below the college composition level) in the mainstream (native-speaker) track, though a parallel course for L2 writers was available. Prior to registration, she was unaware of the multilingual course option but might not have considered it if she had known, given her status as a native-born U.S. citizen (see also Costino & Hyon, 2007).[5]

A text sample (shown and discussed further in Chapter 2) demonstrates that Luciana's writing is more sophisticated than Hector's in both content and rhetorical structure, but her errors are more frequent and more stigmatizing, especially given her status as a non-native speaker of English in a mainstream composition class. Luciana's instructor is a graduate student teaching associate with composition training but no TESOL training. The instructor reported that eight of her 20 students (40 percent) had the same profile as Luciana. This teacher felt unequipped, both in terms of training and time available, to meet those eight students' individual needs, either in or out of class, so she sent the students to the campus Writing Center for one-on-one help. The students were told at the Writing Center that it was "against policy" to give them the sentence-level assistance that they and their teacher were looking for. The teacher, frustrated, asked: "What do we do when the 'ideology' of a program conflicts with the students' actual needs? And how am I supposed to meet the needs of these students with no training and no support?"

These three stories and their student subjects provide a snapshot of the complexity and challenges of educating "non–native English speakers" at English-medium colleges and universities today. The three L2 writers have extremely different backgrounds, and their writing (which will be examined closely in Chapter 2) has features not only different from the writing of native English speakers but from one another. It is also interesting to observe that only one of the three students (John) is enrolled in a specially designated English language or composition course even though all three are easily identifiable from their texts as L2 writers. Finally, the institutional barriers—a graduate writing examination that even a senior such as John was unable to pass, no ESL support options for Hector, an underprepared instructor and no assistance in the writing center for Luciana—are, unfortunately, far too typical and even representative of the experiences of L2 writers at U.S. colleges and universities.

Though John, Hector, and Luciana are real individuals who are at this moment of writing still pursuing their studies in state universities in California, they are also in a sense prototypes of the different "audiences" of L2 writers we are considering. John, of course, is an **international,** or *visa* student, pursuing an American degree with the stated intent of returning to his home country after completing his studies. Hector is a **late-arriving resident** student who moved to the United States, after graduating from high school in his home country, not only for his university studies but to live and work here after completing college. Luciana, born in the United States, is an **early-arriving resident** student, the child of first-generation immigrants. These are the three distinct groups or audiences of second language students at U.S. colleges and universities whom we must consider in our programming, assessment, and instruction.

As more researchers and teachers have become aware of the complexity entailed by the term *second language students* and have turned their attention not only to classification and description but to models of curriculum and instruction that might best (or better) meet these students' needs, some helpful generalizations and issues have emerged. These in turn raise practical questions about how best to support and help those L2 students. Such questions include:

- Should college/university students such as John, Hector, and Luciana receive writing/language instruction or assistance specially designed for L2 students? If so, what kind(s) of assistance?

- What kinds of course placement options and support services are most appropriate and beneficial for an increasingly complex L2 student audience?

- What mechanisms will most successfully identify and place students? Which will be most successful for the greatest number of students?

- Who should teach those students—trained L2 specialists or mainstream writing instructors?
- How should L2 specialists be prepared?
- How can mainstream composition teachers and tutors be better prepared to work with multilingual writers?

Defining the Audiences

A Conceptual Framework

In the recent work on Generation 1.5 students in U.S. higher education, a 1992 paper by Guadalupe Valdés, originally published in *Written Communication* and later reprinted in a 2006 collection (Matsuda, Cox, Jordan, & Ortmeier-Hooper, 2006b), is frequently cited as a starting point. Valdés makes two key distinctions relevant to the discussion in this chapter: (1) elective versus circumstantial bilingualism and (2) incipient versus functional bilingualism (see Fig. 1.2).

Elective bilinguals are "individuals who choose to become bilingual" (Valdés, 1992/2006, p. 37) for some type of personal benefit—education, prestige, career advancement, or travel/cultural opportunities. They "elect" bilingualism by seeking out formal opportunities, such as classes or contexts in which the second language is used. In most cases, international students who come to the United States to pursue an undergraduate or graduate degree (or as exchange students in high school) would fall into the elective bilingual category, as would American students who study a particular foreign language and then travel or study abroad in countries where that language is spoken. In contrast, *circumstantial bilinguals* are those who

> because of their circumstances, find that they must learn another language in order to survive . . . these individuals find themselves in a context in which their ethnic language is not the majority, prestige, or national language. In order to participate economically and politically in the society of which they are a part, such persons must acquire some degree of proficiency in the societal language. (Valdés, 1992/2006, pp. 37–38)

Circumstantial bilinguals might include political refugees to another country or those whose home country has been conquered or colonized (so that another language has become the official language).

As with most dichotomies, there are potential exceptions to these definitions, particularly as they relate to children. In some families, for instance, the parents elect for their children to become bilingual by speaking two languages in the home, by hiring a bilingual caregiver, or by sending their children to a bilingual or immersion

FIGURE 1.2
Defining the Audiences: Key Concepts

Term	Definition
Elective bilingual	One who *chose* to learn or study the L2
Circumstantial bilingual	One who was *required* by life circumstances to learn or study the L2
Incipient bilingual	One who is still an *active learner or acquirer* of the L2
Functional bilingual	One who has acquired a *stable*, possibly fossilized, form of the L2 and *can use it adequately* in many settings or for many purposes
Basic Interpersonal Communication Skills (BICS)	The language needed to function successfully in *everyday settings*
Cognitive Academic Language Proficiency (CALP)	The language needed to function successfully in *academic or professional settings*

Sources: Cummins, 1979; Cummins & Swain, 1986; Valdés, 1992/2006.

school. Valdés specifies that such children "may be considered elective bilinguals if the circumstances requiring the use of two languages are created deliberately by the parents and are not present in the surrounding societal context outside the home" (1992/2006, p. 39). Another possible exception is students in secondary or post-secondary schools who are required to study a foreign language in order to graduate. They have not themselves elected to become bilingual, they cannot elect to refuse, yet it could not be said that they must learn the language for survival. Nonetheless, this fundamental distinction between elective and circumstantial bilinguals is helpful not only as part of our underlying definitions of the different student audiences but also in understanding their differing motivations and the psychological and social issues which accompany them.

The second major distinction made by Valdés is between *incipient* and *functional* bilingualism. She defines *incipient bilingualism* as "the period of acquisition of a second language" (1992/2006, p. 42), immediately admitting that the length of this period is quite variable and determined by a number of disparate factors. Further, some individuals with limited access to native speakers of the L2 and few opportunities to learn it will experience a very long incipient period. Some may never achieve *functional bilingualism*, defined generally as "the ability to use a very broad range of styles and levels in both languages, including the second language" (p. 42). Valdés further observes that "the English of very few of these [functional] bilinguals will be identical to the English of the English-speaking monolinguals," but "no matter how many features remain that are non-nativelike, *there is a point at which an individual must be classified as a functional bilingual* rather than an incipient bilingual" (p. 43, emphasis added). Our third subject profiled, Luciana, would appear to fit this description. Despite her interrupted education and her trips to Mexico with her parents, she was born in the United States and graduated from a U.S. high school. Although her English writing is definitely non-nativelike, she functions well in English in most situations. It would be difficult to argue that she is still an incipient bilingual who belongs in ESL classes.

These basic terms help us not only to understand the complexities of our student population but some of the problems and challenges that exist with identifying them, placing them into appropriate instructional settings, and providing effective assistance to them. For instance, not all international students (most of whom could be considered elective bilinguals) are also *incipient* bilinguals. Some arrive in the United States from English-dominant countries or countries in which English is an official or prominent language (e.g., India or Kenya). Depending on their educational and second language backgrounds, they may be quite functional in English and beyond needing ESL support.

In addition to looking at the nuanced nature of the term *bilingualism,* it is helpful to consider the *type(s)* of language being acquired. Particularly relevant for this book is the famous BICS/CALP distinction made by Cummins (e.g., 1979; Cummins & Swain, 1986). **Basic Interpersonal Communication Skills** (BICS) are acquired naturally in L1 by all children who have no physical or mental impairment. For L2 learners, evidence suggests that BICS can also be acquired in natural, communicative settings in a relatively short time. In contrast, **Cognitive Academic Language Proficiency** (CALP, which includes advanced vocabulary and grammar knowledge as well as strong literacy and critical-thinking skills) takes much longer to develop in both L1 and L2 and in some instances does not develop at all (or adequately) (Collier, 1987, 1989; Scarcella, 1996, 2003). Collier's studies demonstrated that it can take L2 learners at least seven years to develop CALP in L2, even under ideal learning conditions. The BICS/CALP framework further complicates the functional bilingual definition problem, as an L2 learner can appear to be quite functional as to BICS and far less so as to CALP. This seems to be the case for Luciana and Hector and even for John, despite his years of higher education in the United States and English language instruction and exposure in his home country.

With these conceptual distinctions in mind (types or degrees of bilingualism; types of language skills being acquired), we turn to definitions and descriptions of the three groups of L2 learners found in higher education. It is important to state at the outset of this discussion that a number of broad generalizations are necessarily made here. Within each subgroup are major differences in linguistic, cultural, and educational background and experience as well as individual differences in temperament, learning style, self-esteem, motivation, and so forth. However, as a starting point, they provide a helpful frame of reference.

International Students

International Students: Basic Definitions

The first and most traditional student audience is also the easiest to define. **International** students hold student visas to pursue their studies in the United States (or another country) with the stated intent[6] to return to their home countries to live and work upon the completion of their studies (Leki, 1992; Reid, 1997; 1998/2006b). Some pursue bachelor's or graduate degrees to improve their career prospects; others come because more advanced learning opportunities in their field of study are available in the host country (particularly in scientific or technical disciplines). Some students come only for a few months or a year or two to broaden their cultural experience, similar to U.S. undergraduates who take a semester or year abroad. Others come not primarily of their own volition but rather at the request of their government or employer for advanced training and/or language skills. In K–12 settings and even community colleges, this group may further include the children of visiting scholars, of international graduate students, or of foreign workers. What all of these groups have in common is their specific immigration/visa status and the fact that their stay in the L2 country is intended to be *temporary* (with the occasional exception of students from oppressive political regimes hoping to obtain political asylum in the home country) (Leki, 1992). For the most part, these international students would fall into Valdés' (1992/2006) "elective bilingual" category.

International Students: Post-Secondary Context

As already noted, the number of international students in U.S. higher education has grown dramatically over the past half-century. According to the most recent (2007) *Open Doors* report published by the Institute of International Education (IIE), there were 582,984 international students in the United States. International students may be found at virtually all four-year institutions in the United States, but in differing proportions: Doctoral/research institutions have more international students than those that offer only master's, bachelor's, or associate's degrees. The largest sending nations were India, China, Republic of Korea, Japan, Canada, and Taiwan. California was the largest receiving state, followed by New York and Texas. The most commonly selected fields of study are business and management, engineering, physical and life sciences, social sciences, and mathematics and computer sciences, although these percentages vary depending on academic level (undergraduate versus master's versus doctorate) and type of institution. Only about 3 percent pursue majors in the humanities. In addition to students matriculated in degree programs at U.S. colleges and universities, another 45,167 students were granted visas to develop their language skills in Intensive English Programs (IIE, 2007). Nearly all four-year colleges in the United States require that international students demonstrate English language proficiency through submitting scores from the TOEFL® (Test of English as a Foreign Language), which must meet minimum levels that vary from school to school, but exceptions are frequently made for international students who graduated from a U.S. high school or received a U.S. undergraduate degree.

International Students: Characteristics

Because it is expensive and challenging to study abroad, many international students come from relatively privileged and well-educated backgrounds (Reid, 1997; 1998/2006b). In 2007, nearly 62 percent of international students listed their primary source of funding as "personal/family," though the proportions change for graduate students, 46 percent of whom are funded primarily by the U.S. institution at which they are studying (IIE, 2007). Others, however, may be subsisting on a small government allowance or support from families that have sacrificed to send them overseas: "These students live on a meager allowance under a great deal of pressure to finish their expensive educations abroad as quickly as possible" (Leki, 1992, p. 41). Some may be first-generation college students in their families (similar to their immigrant student counterparts). Many are surprised to find after taking an international student or ESL placement examination that they are required to take English language courses prior to or in conjunction with courses in their major field of study. Students under financial pressure may react with anger and panic when they realize that improving their English may delay their graduation and their return home. Others may be so wealthy or influential in their home countries that they expect special treatment from the university and may even arouse the resentment of their usually underpaid ESL instructors.[7]

Generally speaking, international students are hardworking, bright, and motivated. They have been good students in their home countries and are highly proficient and literate in their L1. Because they must obtain minimum TOEFL® scores to gain admission abroad, their English skills, generally learned through years of EFL classes, are fairly proficient. Depending on their country or culture of origin and their prior experiences with foreign travel, they may be experiencing various degrees of culture shock: "They may experience the United States as a veritable Sodom and Gomorrah or, on the other hand, as utterly provincial" (Leki, 1992, p. 41). They may also need time to adjust to an educational system which is quite different from what they are accustomed to. For instance, they may be surprised about the level of informality in American classrooms, that they are expected to attend class regularly and on time and to submit work on a deadline, that attribution of ideas to sources and avoiding plagiarism is an important issue, and that they are expected to formulate opinions and arguments rather than simply summarizing or repeating what they have heard in class or read in the textbook (Aebersold & Field, 1997; Leki, 1992).

International Students: Motivation

Since many international students intend to return to their home countries, their primary cultural identification will be with the home culture. Their desire to assimilate or integrate with U.S. culture may be non-existent or limited, and they may socialize only with other international students, particularly those from the same language and cultural background. However, some more outgoing students may enjoy learning about the host culture, visiting in U.S. homes, and befriending or even dating U.S. residents. Generally speaking, though, international students tend to retain their primary linguistic and cultural identity.

As previously noted, international students as elective bilinguals have usually chosen to study abroad for their personal benefit. They may have very clear ideas about what they want and need to gain from their experience and may resist requirements that strike them as irrelevant to their personal goals. For instance, a student pursuing a degree in science so that he can return to China to become a doctor or to Pakistan to become an engineer may not see the purpose in freshman English requirements or graduation writing requirements. They reason that they will never use English much again (and will certainly never write multiple drafts of an academic English essay), so if they can successfully complete their major coursework, why do they need classes in English composition? This instrumental motivation comes into direct conflict with the values of American post-secondary institutions such as, "A student earning a degree from an American university should be able to demonstrate minimal levels of English/writing proficiency." ESL teachers (especially writing teachers) and administrators should not be surprised by resistance from some international students who may not agree with certain requirements or classroom practices.

Dividing Late-Arriving and Early-Arriving Resident L2 Students

Background

The problem of definition gets much more complicated once we move beyond the international students, who are readily identifiable by their visa status. *Resident* students, broadly speaking, are L2 students who intend to reside permanently in the new country. They may have *permanent resident* ("green card") status, meaning they are legal long-term residents of the United States, or they may be naturalized American citizens. They may also be *undocumented* (illegal) immigrants. They may have come to the new country on their own or with family as adults or they may have come as children accompanying their immigrant parents—or they may be the U.S.-born children of first-generation immigrants. As noted by Matsuda et al. (2006b, p. 1), the 2000 U.S. Census reported 3.5 million foreign-born U.S. residents ages 19–24 and an additional 5.5 million English learners in K–12 public schools. While not all of these immigrants will attend college in the United States, as their numbers and rates of college attendance increase overall, the proportion of foreign-born U.S. residents (or their U.S.-born children) in colleges and universities will also increase (see Matsuda, 2003a; see also Locke, 2007).

There are many different ways to characterize these resident L2 students. As previously noted, changes in U.S. immigration laws and the end of the Vietnam War led to a large wave of immigrants and refugees. These immigrants (or their children) began to make an impact on U.S. higher education by the 1980s, and teachers and scholars began noticing and discussing the differences between international and immigrant ESL students. However, in the 1990s, a different group of immigrants began to appear in larger numbers in post-secondary programs—the children of first-generation immigrants who had grown up and completed all or most of their education in the U.S.—and educators struggled to categorize them. Were they *language minority* or *bilingual* students? Could they properly be called *immigrants* if they had lived here most or even all of their lives? Were they *incipient* bilinguals who belonged in ESL classes, or were they *functional* bilinguals who should be mainstreamed with monolingual native English speakers? In my own institution at that time, we began to notice this third group when they took the in-house exam used to place students in our ESL sequence, and we coined an ad hoc label for them, *NESLs,* which stood for "not ESL." They were non-native speakers of English, but their language abilities, as demonstrated on the exam, did not seem to fit into our traditional ESL program (see also Matsuda, 2008).

Other scholars and educators began to observe the emergence—which happened much earlier and much more dramatically in high-immigration states such as California, Texas, New York, and Florida (Harklau, Siegal, & Losey, 1999)—of this third group, and the use of the term *Generation 1.5* evolved. Rumbaut and Ima (1988), who studied Southeast Asian refugee children in the 1970s and 1980s, are credited with bringing the term into the educational mainstream (Harklau et al., 1999; Roberge, 2002), but as noted by Park (1999) and Roberge (2002), the Korean-American community also has a term in Korean that can be translated as Generation 1.5. Generation 1.5 students are so called because "their experiences, characteristics, and educational needs may lie somewhere between those of *first-generation* adult immigrants and the U.S.-born *second generation* children of immigrants," and the term "denotes these learners' in-between status" (Roberge, 2002, pp. 107–108). As observed by Harklau et al. (1999), when Generation 1.5 students arrive in college "with backgrounds in U.S. culture and schooling, they are distinct from international students or other newcomers . . . while at the same time these students' status as English language learners is often treated as incidental or even misconstrued as underpreparation" (p. 1). Returning to the terms used by Valdés (1992/2006), many of these Generation 1.5 students are clearly functional bilinguals who exhibit non-nativelike features especially in their L2 writing.

While these definitions seem straightforward enough, a problem arises in determining where Generation 1.5 begins and ends. For example, some have narrowly defined Generation 1.5 learners as those who arrive in the United States during the pre-school years (Goen et al., 2002; Roberge, 2002), so that all of their education has been in the United States and in English. Others extend the generation much more broadly to include students who arrived during elementary school, as adolescents, or even as young adults (e.g., Frodesen, 2002; Frodesen & Starna, 1999; Lay, Carro, Tien, Niemann, & Leong, 1999; Leki, 1999; Roberge, 2002; Rodby, 1999, Stegemoller, 2004; Yi, 2007). Some have also included U.S.-born children of first-generation immigrants as part of Generation 1.5 (e.g., Frodesen & Starna, 1999). In a report on the design of a special composition class for Generation 1.5 students at UCLA, Holten (2002) defined the Generation 1.5 group (those eligible for the new course) as "non-native speakers who had been in the U.S. longer than eight years." To the "years in residence" aspect of the definition can also be added where the learners were educated, and for how long (Bosher & Rowekamp, 1998; Reid, 1998/2006b; Seymour & Walsh, 2006): Was their entire education in the United States? Some of it? Did they graduate from high school in the home country or in the United States? Was their education interrupted by time in refugee camps or by moving around with migrant worker parents?

Finally, as noted by Roberge (2002) and others, the demographic and sociocultural dimensions of language minority groups have become increasingly complex. As a result, Roberge argues for "a broad and flexible definition" of Generation 1.5 that "captures the in-between position of many different groups of students whose experiences fall between the poles of 'native' and 'nonnative,' and somewhere between the poles of U.S.-born and newcomer" (2002, p. 109). Others have questioned the term Generation 1.5 altogether (e.g., Schwartz, 2004, who prefers the term *crossover student* to refer to a non–native English speaker who is proficient enough to take mainstream freshman composition courses in college). Finally, one of the most articulate advocates for Generation 1.5 research, Linda Harklau, has recently cautioned against "tendencies to reify the term," fearing that its use will label immigrants as "perpetual foreigners," regardless of how long they have lived in the United States, and become a shorthand for "a discourse of need—a way to label bilingual students as in need of remediation" (Harklau in Matsuda, Canagarajah, Harklau, Hyland & Warschauer, 2003, p. 156). She prefers the use of the term to refer to "active English learners" (probably similar to what Valdés [1992/2006] would call "incipient bilinguals").

Dividing Late and Early Arrivals: Parameters

While "broad and flexible" definitions and warnings appropriately capture the complexity of the bilingual/language minority population, for the purposes of this volume, we will discuss the three L2 student audiences with a bit more precision by sub-dividing the "immigrant" population into **late-arriving** residents and **early-arriving** residents. There are various ways we could divide "early" and "late" arrivals, all of which are somewhat arbitrary, but for the sake of discussion, "early arrivals" are those who have been in the United States longer than eight years.[8]

The "eight years" comes from Holten's (2002) dividing line for the Generation 1.5 writing course at UCLA, as well as from Collier's (1987, 1989) finding that it takes at least seven years to acquire CALP in an L2 (see also the definition provided by Destandau & Wald, 2002). This "early arrival" group will also include **U.S.-born children of first-generation immigrant parents whose primary language was not English**. We will adopt the shorthand **late-arriving students** for the later arrivals and **early-arriving students** for the early arrivals.

It should be noted, however, that there are problems with and exceptions to these group boundaries. Scholars and educators have correctly noted that it is not really a matter of *how long* an immigrant student has been in the United States, but *where and how* they were educated. There may be substantial differences, for example, between a 22-year-old college student who arrived in the United States at age 14—a difficult age developmentally and academically, and on the late side for L2 acquisition—and one who arrived during the pre-school years. Yet the "eight-year" threshold would place both students in the early-arrival group. Thus, it seems helpful to add a second characteristic to this boundary: Early arrivals are those students who have been in the United States for eight years or longer **and who arrived prior to age 10**. Second language acquisition research suggests that, for a variety of cognitive, sociocultural, affective, and academic reasons, younger arrivals have better long-term L2 acquisition success (e.g., Pienemann & Johnson, 1987). While certainly not perfect, these two criteria for dividing early and late arrivals (number of years in the United States and age at arrival) will give us a clearer picture of the distinctions among students in these two categories.

Late-Arriving Resident Students

Late-Arriving Students: Post-Secondary Contexts

Unlike international students who must present evidence of English language proficiency to gain admission to U.S. colleges, **late-arriving** students may have studied little or no English prior to coming to the United States. As a result, some may attend adult education ESL programs offered through K–12 or community college districts and/or low-level community college courses. Depending on where they live, they may also take classes and obtain services at refugee or community service centers designed for immigrants of their linguistic and cultural background. Their K–12 children may attend newcomer schools if available and then regular public schools, which may or may not offer bilingual education or ESL instruction. Adult immigrants wishing to obtain further education will typically choose community colleges, which are relatively inexpensive, tend to have extensive ESL and/or remedial English offerings, and offer open admissions and the opportunity to transfer later to a four-year public university. As for four-year institutions, it is more likely that late-arriving students will attend state universities focused on undergraduate teaching rather than public research universities or private colleges.

While some highly motivated and financially stable immigrant students may indeed pursue degrees at these more prestigious institutions,[9] most late-arriving students do not have the financial means, the confidence, or the English language skills to attempt such a challenging path.

Late-Arriving Students: Characteristics

The literature on post-1965 immigration refers to *voluntary immigrants,* or those who came to the United States for greater opportunity following the loosening of immigration laws, and *refugees,* or those fleeing political or religious oppression or persecution. As a result of these distinctions, some late-arriving students may be financially well off (indeed, in some instances, they are required to demonstrate their self-sufficiency to be approved for immigration) while others have no money of their own and must be supported by relatives or receive public assistance in order to survive. Many work long hours at multiple jobs to survive and support their families, which in some cultural groups are quite large. Those who do attempt to attend college are often distracted or burdened by these financial and familial responsibilities, which can hinder their academic and L2 progress (Harklau, Siegal, & Losey, 1999; Lay et al., 1999; Rodby, 1999).

While there certainly is variation among international students in terms of academic talent, prior educational success, work ethic, and so forth, there is much more so among the late-arriving resident student population. Whether they are voluntary immigrants or refugees, there is tremendous diversity in prior educational achievement, L1 proficiency, and L2 ability. Some may have been well-educated professionals in their home countries; others may have had limited or interrupted schooling. Some may be highly proficient and fully literate in the L1 while others may have strong L1 BICS but limited CALP—and some may not be literate in the L1 at all. Many will have had exposure and/or education in the English language prior to coming to the United States, but others may have had little or none. Like international students, newly arrived residents may experience various degrees and stages of culture shock (Goen et al., 2002). James (1997) notes that immigrant children and adolescents in schools may be among the most at risk for psycho-social problems, including adjustment to the school system itself, interactions with peers, and increasing distance or alienation from their parents and home culture (see also Roberge, 2002).

Late-Arriving Students: Motivation

Because late-arriving immigrants intend to reside permanently in the L2 country, in general they are interested in learning about the culture and becoming assimilated into society. Again, however, there is variation depending on whether they live in a linguistic enclave with others from their native country or language background and also on the degree of difference between their home culture and American culture. For example, conservative Christians who came to the United States to escape religious persecution may be horrified at what they consider the relative permissiveness or immorality in this culture and be very intentional about keeping themselves distinct from it—and may even openly express hostility toward lifestyles and value systems with which they disagree (Leki, 1992). However, the longer they remain in the United States, the more familiar and comfortable they become with the surrounding culture, and this increased awareness facilitates their language acquisition on several different levels.

In academic settings, late-arriving resident students may be more easily convinced of the long-term benefits of improving their L2 reading and writing skills, building vocabulary, and improving grammar and pronunciation. Unlike many of their international student counterparts, they plan to live and work in the new country (Hartman & Tarone, 1999; Raimes, 1991). This difference in motivation and goals may mean that immigrant students in language classes might be more receptive to requirements or suggestions about extensive reading in the L2, writing fluently and accurately, and learning more about the target language. For them, the L2 is not just a means to a short-term end but rather a key to their future success and that of their children.

Early-Arriving Resident Students

Early-Arriving Students: Post-Secondary Contexts

Because early-arriving students were raised and sometimes born in this country, they can increasingly be found in all educational contexts. In some states, such as California and New York, their presence in the K–12 school system and in community colleges has already had a significant and profound impact, one that will continue to grow as their numbers increase in proportion to the rest of the population (Bosher & Rowekamp, 1998; Harklau et al., 1999; Lay et al., 1999; Locke, 2007; Paral, 2008; Roberge, 2002; Schrag, 2008).

As noted by Harklau, Siegal, and Losey (1999), "Because U.S. colleges and universities collect virtually no information about U.S. residents' or citizens' native language status, we cannot say exactly how many [bilingual English learners] there are" (p. 4; see also Browning et al., 2000). However, counting not only incipient bilinguals (those who would be officially classified as ESL or English learners) but late-arriving and early-arriving L2 students at various stages of functional bilingualism, Harklau et al. (1999) estimated that there may be as many as 225,000 English learners graduating from U.S. high schools each year—and increasingly, many of those continue on to college.[10] As with late-arriving students, there are probably more early-arriving L2 students in community colleges and state teaching universities than in private colleges or public research universities (Blanton, 1999). However, given the size, diversity, and complexity of the group called early-arriving students, it is also likely that there are more students from this group at more elite institutions than there are late-arriving resident students (see Locke, 2007, for a recent report on resident immigrant students at the University of California).

Early-Arriving Students: Characteristics

Early-arriving students are most typically the children of first-generation immigrants. Many of those immigrant parents live in modest circumstances and must work hard at relatively unskilled and low-paying jobs to support their families. The parents also tend to know less English than do their U.S.-educated children. However, some immigrant parents are well off and well educated, and they tend to instill their work ethic and respect for education into their children. Early-arriving L2 children who grew up in less privileged circumstances likely also attended schools with fewer resources to support their academic development in general and their English language acquisition in particular. Some early-arriving students attended bilingual or ESL programs in elementary school; by middle school, many were reclassified as English proficient and placed in mainstream classes with monolingual English speakers (Browning et al., 2000; Roberge, 2002; Schrag, 2008). Most early-arriving students have acquired BICS in the L1 but do not become fully or even minimally literate in it (Browning et al., 2000; Chiang & Schmida, 1999; Harklau, 2003; Harklau et al., 1999; Singhal, 2004). The dominant *academic* language is the L2.

The educational outcomes for early-arriving students become more problematic to trace as they reach secondary levels. Some students have become fully functional bilinguals by that point, and they do well enough in mainstream classes. Many, however, are still in the process of L2 acquisition when they are reclassified (Browning et al., 2000). The mainstreaming produces the unfortunate effect of requiring them to meet increasingly complex and difficult academic demands while competing with monolingual native speakers and with no accommodation made for their status as continuing language learners (Hartman & Tarone, 1999; Miramontes, 1993; Roberge, 2002). Those who do graduate from high school and go on to college have often done so through taking a combination of courses that required fairly minimal language production and remedial English/ESL classes that were fairly mechanical (focused on grammar and controlled composition) and in which their classmates were non-standard variety speakers or had behavior or other learning problems. Because the early-arriving L2 students are considered "the good kids," they tend to perform well in these classes (Harklau, 2000), but the classes often fall far short of providing them with the academic language skills they will need in college (Frodesen, 2002; Hartman & Tarone, 1999; Lay et al., 1999; Leki, 1999; Muchisky & Tangren, 1999; Olsen, 1997; Roberge, 2002).

Early-Arriving Students: Motivation

Early-arriving L2 students, having lived in the United States for most or all of their lives, have by far the greatest level of cultural awareness and assimilation of the three L2 student groups. In many ways they look and act like any other American teenager or young adult. However, studies of the social, linguistic, and cultural self-identification of early-arriving students paint a much more complicated picture (Chiang & Schmida, 1999; Nero, 1997). Students may self-identify as American, as whatever their parents' cultural label is (e.g., "Hmong"), or as a hyphenate ("Hmong-American"). When asked what their "first" language is, they may reply with their parents' L1 (the language they first heard as young children in the home), with English, or with confusion, not exactly sure what is meant by "first" ("Dominant"? "Used most frequently"? "Most important"? "The language I speak with my parents? With my friends? At home? At school?"). Early-arriving students tend to identify strongly with their parents, including their home language and culture, but they also desire to fit into the surrounding culture they have always known. In terms of cultural and linguistic identity, they are truly "in-between," as implied when the Generation 1.5 label is used to describe them. However, again, there is a great deal of variation within this early-arriving group (Roberge, 2002). For example, students living in linguistic enclaves or in transnational families (such as our profile subject Luciana) may be less assimilated and comfortable with American culture than an early-arriving student who grew up in a monolingual English or culturally diverse neighborhood or school system.

There is also a bit of internal confusion caused by the application of either the Generation 1.5 or early-arriving label to U.S.-born children of first-generation immigrants, as those children are technically second generation. Previous research on immigration and assimilation patterns presented certain conclusions about second- (and third- and fourth-) generation immigrants, most notably each generation's increasing distance or even alienation from the home language and culture of the first generation. These generalizations appear to be somewhat less true for the late-20th-century immigrants, who for a variety of social and cultural reasons seem to assimilate more slowly and in many cases have a more difficult time acquiring English (McKay & Wong, 2000). It should also be noted that in many families, older siblings may be immigrants (born in the parents' home country) while the younger ones are U.S.-born. These siblings share every relevant linguistic, cultural, and environmental characteristic, so it makes sense to refer to all of the children of first-generation immigrants as being part of the early-arriving student group, regardless of birthplace or citizenship status.

Like the late-arriving residents, early-arriving students are motivated to learn English and succeed academically for the simple reason that they will live out their lives in the new country, so in order to survive and thrive, they must achieve linguistic and academic proficiency. Because early-arriving L2 students spend most or all of their years of education in American schools, their expectations are similar to those of other native-born English speakers, and like any other group of students, they will display a range of behavior patterns and attitudes toward their schooling. When they get to college, they are less likely than the other two groups to segregate themselves into fields of study that require relatively little English

FIGURE 1.3

Basic Comparisons of the Three Audiences

Characteristic	International	Late-Arriving Immigrant	Early-Arriving Immigrant
Literate in L1	Yes	Maybe	Maybe
Primary cultural identification	L1	Mostly L1	L2
Knowledge of L2 culture	No	Some	Yes
L2 literacy experience	Limited	Limited	Extensive (but not always effective)
Socioeconomic status	Upper-middle-class to wealthy	Working class	Working to middle class
Motivation to learn English	For instrumental purposes	For integrative and survival purposes	Like monolingual English speakers

(e.g., scientific and technical majors), and these early arrivals may be found in any and all degree programs available at the particular institution.

As the previous discussion demonstrates, L2 students at colleges and universities today can vary from one another dramatically. Indeed, perhaps their only real similarities are that they began life speaking another language and have been exposed to at least two different cultures. Figure 1.3 summarizes the basic differences across the three groups (see also Friedrich, 2006, and Matsuda, 2008, for similar schemes).

As will be shown in Chapter 2, these differences also affect the three student audiences' academic progress and especially their English language/literacy development. Once the differing academic language needs of the different L2 student audiences have been examined, we can begin to address the types of programs and curricula that might best serve each group (Chapters 3 and 6) and the ways in which classroom instruction can be sensitive and responsive to the differences across groups (Chapters 4 and 5).

QUESTIONS FOR REFLECTION AND DISCUSSION

1. Before reading this chapter, were you aware that the number of L2 students in colleges and universities has increased so dramatically—and become so diverse—in the past 50 years? Did the information presented confirm impressions you already had or did some of it surprise you—and if so, what and how?

2. As you read the profiles of John, Hector, and Luciana, what struck you, stood out to you, or concerned you? Have you known any students like them, and what are the similarities and differences between your acquaintances and these three prototypes?

3. After "Three Stories," several practical questions or implications that this book aims to examine and address are given (see pages 8–9). Choose one or more of these questions, and make some notes about your own opinions, observations, or experiences with the issue(s) raised. Keep your notes and review them once you have read the later chapters.

4. An extended discussion is included about how to define or differentiate between students who are late-arriving resident immigrants and those who are in the early-arriving group. What is your opinion about the ways in which those lines are drawn (see also Chapter 1, Endnote 8)? Would you define the groups differently? Would you add more categories?

5. The final section of this chapter defined and described three distinct L2 student groups (international, late-arriving, and early-arriving students) across several different sub-categories, such as institutions, motivation, etc. Are these (admittedly generalized) "portraits" essentially accurate in your opinion, observation, and experience? If not, how might you change or adjust them?

CHAPTER ENDNOTES

[1] In this volume I cite two distinct pieces of work: Harklau, Losey, & Siegal (1999), which refers to those authors' efforts as editors of a collection, and Harklau, Siegal, & Losey (1999), which refers to their introductory chapter of that collection. Because of the potential for confusion, I will refer to the edited collection after first mention as "Harklau et al." and to the individual chapter as "Harklau, Siegal, & Losey."

[2] See also the historical analysis of Matsuda and Matsuda (2009), which points out that the presence of resident ESL writers in U.S. universities was "noticed" by the mid-1950s (Slager, 1956).

[3] As another indicator, a recent report (Paral, 2008) based on U.S. census data notes that 49 percent of the children ages 12–17 in California have at least one immigrant parent.

[4] I am grateful to my former student Lisa Henry Clark for her permission to use her profile of John in this chapter, to Cara Tupper for her profile of Hector, and to Ann Michaels for her profile of Luciana.

[5] In this particular program, there are parallel courses for ESL/multilingual students. While some U.S.-born L2 students choose these multilingual sections, others prefer to take the mainstream composition equivalent, feeling that they left ESL courses behind years ago in elementary or middle school.

[6] As noted by one of the reviewers, international students *must* have a stated intent to return to their home countries in order to obtain a U.S. visa—but they may nonetheless privately intend to stay permanently if possible.

[7] Some years ago, I taught international graduate students at a private university in Los Angeles who paid more every year in car insurance than I had paid for my car and who thought nothing of going to Las Vegas for the weekend and gambling away $35,000!

[8] One of my survey respondents (see Chapter 6) took issue with my definitions here, arguing that the dividing line between "immigrant" (or late-arriving) and "Generation 1.5" (or early-arriving) should be whether or not the student graduated from a U.S. high school. While this would be a legitimate categorizing scheme, I would note that a student who arrives in the United States during high school (say at age 15 or so) and begins college at age 18 or 19 may still have major language/literacy challenges despite having graduated from a U.S. high school—challenges different from those faced by U.S. residents who were born here or who completed all or most of their schooling in English.

[9] See Destandau & Wald, 2002; Frodesen, 2002; Frodesen & Starna, 1999; Holten, 2002; Locke, 2007; Scarcella, 1996, 2003 for discussions of immigrant and Generation 1.5 students at various University of California campuses; see Leki, 1995, 1999 for discussions of students at the University of Tennessee; see Blanton, 1999, 2005, for discussion of students at the private University of New Orleans and other prestigious universities.

[10] In his *Sacramento Bee* column, Schrag (2008) notes that 43 percent of the students currently in California's K–12 public schools started out "speaking some other language." Though some are still officially classified as *English learners* and others have been redesignated as *fully English proficient,* the numbers demonstrate that a substantial percentage of students have experiences with or pathways to English different from that of the mainstream students. Though these percentages are much higher in California than anywhere else, they nonetheless underscore the urgency for schools, colleges, and universities to understand and better serve this increasingly diverse student audience.

Chapter 2

Academic Language and Literacy and the Different L2 Student Audiences

... the widespread expectation that adult language learners can attain completely monolingual-like command of an L2 is unrealistic and only possible in a nation that is overwhelmingly monolingual.

—Harklau, Siegal, & Losey, 1999, p. 8

Chapter 1 identified three distinct audiences of L2 students currently represented in U.S. colleges and universities, provided some basic definitions of each group, and looked at their general characteristics. Three student prototypes—John, Hector, and Luciana, who represent the **international, late-arriving resident, and early-arriving resident** L2 student groups respectively—were introduced. Chapter 2 examines what is known about each student group and their particular strengths, weaknesses, and needs as they attempt as L2 learners to negotiate post-secondary education and its increasingly complex academic language demands.

As a conceptual framework for this discussion, consider the construct of "academic language" and its important subset, "academic literacy." What types of knowledge and skills do *all* higher education students need to possess and master, regardless of linguistic status? How are these skills particularly challenging for *all* English learners, whether they are international, late-arriving resident, or early-arriving resident students? Do L2 learners differ across the three audiences with regard to linguistic knowledge and academic skills, and if so, in what ways? Chapter 2 also looks specifically at several aspects of academic language proficiency: linguistic knowledge (especially grammar and vocabulary), academic oral/aural abilities (such as listening comprehension, interaction, fluency, and pronunciation), and academic literacy (reading/writing abilities). In this chapter, we learn more about the three prototypes, examining brief text samples from each student as a way to illustrate their shared challenges as well as their differences.

Academic Language: An Overview

As discussed in Chapter 1 (see Fig. 1.2), Cummins (1979; Cummins & Swain, 1986) articulated a helpful distinction between everyday language (BICS) and the language needed in academic settings (CALP). However, as noted by Scarcella (2003), this basic dichotomy does not describe "academic language" in ways precise enough to help teachers. The development of CALP involves increased progress in several interacting dimensions identified by Kern (2000), developed further by Scarcella (2003), and operationalized as to academic writing by Singhal (2004). They are summarized in Figure 2.1.

Linguistic Dimension

In order to read in an L2, mastery of the written system (in English, the Roman alphabet) and knowledge of its sound/symbol correspondences is needed, as well as understanding of spelling patterns and conventions and awareness that words can be spelled similarly and have related meanings but have differences in pronunciation across word classes (e.g., *photograph, photography*). Lexical knowledge includes the ability to recognize and appropriately use frequently occurring words in addition to a large "general" academic vocabulary (Coxhead, 2000, 2006; Folse, 2004, 2008; Nation, 2001) and language that is specific to particular disciplines. It also includes an understanding of English patterns of homonymy (two words pronounced

FIGURE 2.1

Dimensions of Academic Language Proficiency

Dimension	Elements
Linguistic	• Phonological • Lexical • Grammatical • Sociolinguistic • Discourse
Cognitive	• Knowledge • Higher-order thinking • Strategies • Metalinguistic awareness
Sociocultural/psychological	• Social and cultural norms, values, beliefs, attitudes, motivations, interests, behaviors, practices, and habits; these vary cross-culturally

Sources of framework: Kern, 2000; Scarcella, 2003.

identically but with different meanings and possibly different spellings), synonymy (two different words with the same meaning), and polysemy (multiple meanings for the same word) (see also Birch, 2007; Coxhead, 2006; Folse, 2004, 2008; and Koda, 2004 for further discussion of the challenges for L2 learners involved in mastering English vocabulary).

Grammatical competence includes recognition (for reading) and mastery (for writing) of basic sentence patterns, basic verb tenses, plurals, articles, and subject-verb agreement; for academic discourse, it also includes the ability to interpret and produce passives, parallel structures, conditionals, complex clauses (e.g., relative and adjective clauses), different types of reference, and modal auxiliaries (Byrd & Bunting, 2008; Conrad, 2008; Coxhead & Byrd, 2007; Hinkel, 2002, 2004; Scarcella, 2003; Seymour & Walsh, 2006); for writing, it further requires understanding of punctuation rules to combine phrases, clauses, and sentences (Singhal, 2004).

The sociolinguistic component of linguistic knowledge includes a variety of issues such as

- varying language appropriately for different audiences (friends versus professors, formal versus informal)

- the ability to carry out everyday social tasks such as apologizing, complaining, or requesting

- the ability to carry out academic tasks such as defining, explaining, and justifying

- the use of cohesion (linguistic devices that link ideas such as pronoun reference, conjunction, synonyms, etc.) to follow ideas in a text (for reading) and provide signals to a reader (for writing)

- understanding the purpose and structure of complicated academic genres (e.g., abstracts, research articles, dissertations) and knowledge of general modes of discourse such as narration, persuasion, compare and contrast, cause and effect, and so forth (Scarcella, 2003; Singhal, 2004)

Finally, the discourse component also includes clear beginnings and endings to texts, orderly presentation of ideas, and balance of ideas (equivalent coverage of various points and sections of a text).

It should be evident that the linguistic dimension of academic language alone presents many challenges to L2 students attempting to function academically. The vast majority of L2 students in higher education cannot approach the everyday lexical knowledge of their native-speaking counterparts, let alone master the general and specialized vocabulary they will need to function academically (Aebersold & Field, 1997; Birch, 2007; Conrad, 2008; Coxhead, 2000, 2006; Folse, 2004, 2008; Hinkel, 2002; Hudson, 2007; Koda, 2004; Nation, 2001; Silva, 1993). Even functional bilinguals will sometimes have "fossilized" features in their writing and speaking that mark them as being non-native (Frodesen & Starna, 1999; Valdés, 1992/2006).

Cognitive Dimension

It is daunting enough to consider the linguistic component of academic language and the challenges it presents to L2 learners. However, the picture becomes even more complex when one considers the cognitive dimension. This dimension, as outlined in Figure 2.1, also includes several different components. The first, *knowledge,* concerns students' background knowledge (or *schema/schemata*) as it applies to learning new content and reading new texts as well as approaching unfamiliar communicative situations (speaking and writing). For example, students who learn or understand how college-level textbooks tend to be structured can develop strategies to read them more effectively—for instance by carefully previewing the text through examination of the table of contents and the author's preface or by looking at the beginning and/or end of the chapter for a preview or summary of its main points.

Another component of the cognitive dimension is the *critical-thinking* component, which includes such practical skills as interpreting, evaluating, and synthesizing claims; determining the credibility of sources; considering "extra" material such as cartoons, illustrations, graphs, and charts in overall meaning; understanding what is stated and noting what is not stated; and distinguishing between fact and opinion (Scarcella, 2003). Higher-order thinking in production (speaking and writing) consists minimally of selecting and balancing relevant ideas; supporting a thesis, remaining focused on it and referring back to it; critical analysis of issues raised by other sources; countering or delimiting opposing viewpoints; and providing the appropriate amount of background information. Most educators at secondary and post-secondary levels talk about the importance of developing students' critical-thinking skills, but it should also be noted that in practice, these skills are not always emphasized (see Leki, 1999, for a thoughtful discussion of this point).

The *strategic* component of the cognitive dimension can be defined as "the steps we take to make sure that we are comprehending and communicating effectively." For reading, being strategic might include underlining, highlighting, or annotating texts in margins; outlining the entire text during or after reading; effectively using the dictionary; identifying key ideas; and using context and word analysis strategies to determine meaning. In writing, the strategic component might include brainstorming, comparing one's own experiences with other texts, providing examples, citing experiences and observations, and providing evidence from other sources. Finally, the *metalinguistic awareness* component can be characterized as "the ability to think about language use and to fall back on learned knowledge about language." For writers, metalinguistic awareness might come into play during various stages of the writing process, as they call upon rhetorical knowledge (of terms such as *thesis, topic sentence, counterargument, transitions,* etc.) and grammatical knowledge for editing (this could also include mechanical issues such as punctuation and capitalization).

Sociocultural/Psychological Dimension

This final element acknowledges that there are socially and culturally influenced values, beliefs, behaviors, motivations, and practices that affect academic endeavors—and that these vary cross-culturally: "learners' value systems frequently come into conflict with values associated with academic communities" (Gee, 1996, cited in Scarcella, 2003, p. 30). Examples of such cultural value clashes might include L2 students' tendency to provide too much summary and not enough critical analysis; to be unable to ask professors for support or assistance; and to be too tentative or apologetic in making requests (or too aggressive, in some instances). I once received an email from a graduate student in another country that expressed admiration for one of my articles and a wish to travel to Sacramento to study with me—and was signed, "Lots of love"! Though I was amused by this, it also did not inspire me to make arrangements for her to come and work with me as a visiting scholar. Similarly, I received an email from an early-arriving student at my own institution that began, "Hey FERRIS!"—again, amusing, but hardly appropriate.

Academic Language: Summary

Building on the dimensions outlined by Kern (2000) and Scarcella (2003), Singhal (2004) further outlines the types of skills all students must develop to function in academic settings, subdividing them under "communication skills," "critical thinking skills," and "research skills" (pp. 8–10). It is clear from all of these discussions that the development of academic language/literacy proficiency is a challenging endeavor for all students, and particularly those functioning in an L2. Returning to Cummins' BICS/CALP distinction, it is important to observe that many L1 students also do not adequately develop CALP; this is why there are so many students who need remediation when they enter college and why these at-risk students often do not complete their degrees, even at the associate (two-year) level.[1] L2 students are at an even greater disadvantage in developing academic language skills, as they had a later start than L1 peers as to the linguistic dimension, their prior educational experiences may have failed to develop their critical-thinking skills, and their social/cultural norms and values may differ from those of "mainstream" L1 students.

The Three L2 Student Audiences and Academic Language/Literacy Skills

Having argued that academic language proficiency is a challenging goal for *all* students, especially L2 learners, we turn to the three different groups of L2 students defined in Chapter 1 to examine the distinctions among them with regard to academic language development. This discussion will include the subtopics of formal language knowledge, oral/aural communication, reading, and writing. For each, the relative strengths, weaknesses, challenges, and needs presented by the three L2 audiences will be outlined. It is important to remember that within each of these groups is considerable variation; these generalizations are helpful but do not apply equally to all students and contexts.

Formal vs. Everyday Language Knowledge: "Eye" Learners

Reid (1997, 2006a, 1998/2006b) outlines a helpful distinction between "eye" and "ear" learners of English (see Figure 2.2). "Eye" learners are defined as those who are

> literate and fluent in their first language, and they have learned English principally through their **eyes**, studying vocabulary, verb forms, and language rules. These students know, understand, and can explain English grammar; they have usually learned grammar through methodologies that focus on rule learning. (Reid, 1998/2006b, p. 79; see also Kroll, 1990a)

Most **international** students would fall into the category of "eye" learners, although Reid notes that there are some exceptions: "international students who come to the U.S. to study because they have not been successful in their own educational system, and/or whose study of both their first language and English has been limited" (1998/2006b, p. 80). It is also important to note that among international students from a range of countries there may be tremendous variation as to formal language knowledge depending on the L2 methodology or approach used in their home countries. In other words, while it is often taken as axiomatic that all international students have a strong foundation in English grammar and in some cases can explain grammar rules better than their native-speaking ESL

FIGURE 2.2
"Eye" and "Ear" Learners

Type of Learner	Definition	Student Audience
Eye	Primary route to English **learning** was through formal classroom language study	International Some late-arriving resident students
Ear	Primary route to English **acquisition** was through naturalistic exposure to language	Other late-arriving residents Early-arriving residents

See also Reid, 1997, 2006a, 1998/2006b; see also Krashen, 1982; Krashen & Terrell, 1983.

teachers are able to, this is a sweeping generalization that does not apply equally well to all so-called eye learners. However, it probably *is* fair to say that in most cases international students' formal/metalinguistic knowledge surpasses that of either late- or early-arriving resident students.

Formal Vocabulary Study

An important aspect of formal language knowledge is intentional vocabulary learning. As noted by Reid (1998/2006b), "eye" learners have intentionally studied L2 vocabulary in their English classes. Also, because of their strong L1 foundation, they may know more vocabulary in general and academic vocabulary in particular and have acquired a range of literacy skills, including the ability to use word analysis techniques and context to gain a sense of new lexical items they encounter. Whether or not any of their L1 vocabulary knowledge includes L2 cognates, this prior acquisition of vocabulary and experience with learning it through exposure to texts gives "eye" learners an advantage in grappling with the lexical demands of the academic register. Nonetheless, L2 vocabulary knowledge (or the lack thereof) is a problem for *all* L2 learners in academic settings, including international students ("eye" learners or "elective bilinguals"). This point is discussed later in this chapter (see also Chapters 4–5).

Some late-arriving immigrant students may also fall primarily into the "eye" learner category if they arrived in the L2 culture in late adolescence or adulthood, had a relatively complete L1 education, and studied English formally in their home country. These late-arriving immigrants may also continue their formal English language study in newcomer schools, adult schools, or intensive ESL programs upon arrival in the new country. The key issue in this eye/ear distinction is not students' immigration/visa status but rather the nature of their learning experiences in the L2 together with the extent of their education in the L1.

Formal vs. Everyday Language Knowledge: "Ear" Learners

In contrast to "eye" learners, Reid (1998/2006b) says of "ear" learners that they are

> orally fluent in their first language, but due to limited or interrupted schooling, they may not be fully literate in that language. These students have learned English by being suddenly immersed in the language and culture of the U.S. Specifically, they have acquired English principally through their **ears:** They listened, took in oral language (from teachers, TV, grocery clerks, friends, peers) and subconsciously began to form vocabulary, grammar, and syntax rules, learning English principally through oral trial and error. (p. 77)

"Ear" learners as described by Reid would typically fall into Valdés' (1992/2006) "circumstantial bilingual" category. Most late-arriving resident students, with the exception of those described previously, and all early-arriving students could be categorized as "ear" learners of English. For the most part, they learned English informally and naturalistically, in school, on the playground, with peers outside of school, and in the surrounding environment. While some may have had ESL and/or English grammar instruction as part of their K–12 education, generally speaking, "grammar has often been ignored or under-emphasized in public school instruction" (Scarcella, 2003, p. 61), though there is some evidence that this trend is changing (e.g., the 1998 California State Standards for Language Arts Instruction). "Ear" learners typically will not be able to identify or recognize parts of speech, could not articulate grammar rules, and would not recognize grammar terms or rules if used by their teachers in error correction (Ferris, 1999, 2002, 2006; Ferris & Roberts, 2001; Reid, 2006a, 1998/2006b).

"Ear" Learners: Vocabulary Knowledge

As to vocabulary knowledge, ear learners, particularly those who have lived in the L2 environment for many years, have both advantages and disadvantages when compared with eye learners. They have the advantage of broader and deeper cultural knowledge and more opportunities for interaction with other speakers of the L2 and various types of input in and exposure to the target language itself. These assets help them to develop a sound foundation in general, everyday vocabulary, and aural comprehension skills that help them continue to learn the language. On the other hand, they have limited or no literacy in L1 and may have underdeveloped literacy skills and experience in L2. As already noted, prior literacy experience in any language is an advantage for academic literacy development in general and growth in lexical knowledge in particular (Bosher & Rowekamp, 1998; Cummins, 1979; Leki, Cumming, & Silva, 2006; Muchisky & Tangren, 1999, but see Birch, 2007, and Koda, 2004, for caveats with regard to cross-linguistic interference in L2 lexical acquisition).

The "eye/ear" learner distinction outlined by Reid (1997, 2006a, 1998/2006b) specifically to discuss differences among L2 writers is also reminiscent of the "acquisition/learning hypothesis" posed by Krashen (e.g., 1982; Krashen & Terrell, 1983). Krashen defines L2 *acquisition* as what happens naturally and unconsciously through exposure to "comprehensible input" in the L2, while L2 *learning* occurs consciously and formally and usually in a classroom. Krashen argues that acquisition processes or experiences are more beneficial and successful for long-term L2 development and claims that there is only a limited and greatly constrained role for formal learning (the "Monitor" hypothesis). Though there has been a great deal of argument among scholars about Krashen's acquisition/learning hypothesis, it effectively captures the fact that there are two distinct routes to language acquisition and that they appear to produce different types of knowledge about language (and the ability to use it).

However, it may be the case that *academic* language is so complex that mastering it requires formal explanation and consciously focused attention (i.e., "eye" learning). It has been acknowledged that the lexical, syntactic, and rhetorical information contained in academic discourse is not readily available in everyday language, in literary texts, or in light pleasure reading (Biber, 1988, 2006; Coxhead, 2006; Coxhead & Byrd, 2007; Cummins, 1979; Day & Bamford, 1998; Krashen, 2004). Perhaps natural language acquisition and immersion in the L2 environment is the most beneficial way to acquire BICS—but CALP is best developed in school. This distinction may help to explain the counterintuitive finding that L2 students who are the most successful academically are not always the ones who have lived in the L2-dominant country the longest but rather those who are highly proficient and literate in their L1 and/or who have developed substantial academic literacy skills in any language (Bosher & Rowekamp, 1998; Harklau et al., 1999; Leki, Cumming, & Silva, 2006; Muchisky & Tangren, 1999).

Distinctions among "Ear" Learners

All that said, it is necessary to distinguish further among the "ear" learners who are late-arriving residents and those who are early-arriving students. Although there is tremendous individual variation, it is probably fair to say that the early-arriving students as a group have more *acquired* L2 knowledge—more intuitions about how the language operates—than the late-arriving ear learners who have been in residence only a few years. In other words, the language of early-arriving students is more like that of monolingual native English speakers than is the language of other late-arriving resident students (and for that matter, of international "eye" learners). Early arrivals for the most part have had more exposure to the L2 over a longer period of time beginning at a younger age, so they have developed to a greater degree the "felt sense" of the language that allows them to produce more target-like utterances in the first place and to be able to self-correct errors (based on intuition, not formal grammar knowledge) when given the opportunity to do so. However, considering Roberge's (2002) detailed breakdown of different types of Generation 1.5 learners, it is important to note that early-arriving students raised in linguistic enclaves, transnational students, and those who acquired a non-standard form of English from other functional bilinguals (Valdés, 1992/2006) may be exceptions to the generalization that early-arriving students as a group possess a superior degree of acquired intuitions about the L2. In sum, generally speaking, the international student audience has the most *formal knowledge* of grammar, the early-arriving resident group has the strongest *acquired intuitions* about the L2, and the late-arriving resident group is between the two ends of the "eye/ear" learner continuum.

Specific Language Skills: Listening/Speaking

At the college/university level, oral/aural L2 proficiency tends to get the least attention from researchers and materials/curriculum developers (Ferris & Tagg, 1996a, 1996b; Flowerdew, 1994; Murphy, 2006). Educators outside of the ESL realm tend to place more importance on academic literacy (reading/writing) skills. Most four-year university ESL programs thus focus heavily or exclusively on academic literacy (especially writing) development; it is unusual for ESL oral skills classes to be offered at all, and when such courses do exist (e.g., International Teaching Assistant training courses; electives in public speaking, accent reduction, conversation, or listening comprehension), they almost never provide graduation credit. Two-year colleges in the United States tend to have more well-rounded ESL programs, and their offerings often include listening/speaking courses (but again, often not transferable to a degree program).

Others have noted a distinction between international and U.S. resident students with regard to oral skills. The generalization typically made is that "international students are often much better in reading and writing English than in comprehending or speaking it, particularly when they first arrive in an English-speaking country" (Leki, 1992, p. 43) and that "their listening and oral skills are hampered by lack of experience, nonnative English-speaking teachers [in the home country], and the culture shock that comes from being in a foreign culture, the language of which sounds like so much 'noise,' so different from their studied English language" (Reid, 1998/2006b, p. 79). In contrast, "many immigrant or permanent resident students are quite proficient speakers of English" (Leki, 1992, p. 43) and they have "relatively developed English oral fluency and listening skills" (Reid, 1998/2006b, p. 77).

International Students' Academic Oral Skills

Researchers have identified specific struggles that international students may experience with the oral/aural demands of studying abroad. American lecturing styles are often more informal than in other countries (Dudley-Evans, 1994; Flowerdew, 1994; Mason, 1994), so students educated elsewhere may have to adjust their expectations. In smaller classes, newly arrived students must learn how to cope successfully with the "lecture-discussion" model of teaching, which may be a combination of formal lecture, student questions and comments, the instructor's informal responses to student input, and student responses to one another (Ferris, 1998; Ferris & Tagg, 1996a; Lynch, 1994; Mason, 1994).

Another area of difficulty is oral class participation. Students may feel anxiety about their non-native accents and worry that their instructors and peers will be irritated by them (Ferris, 1998; Ferris & Tagg, 1996a). Even in graduate seminars, international students may feel uncomfortable with taking the floor in discussions, instead preferring to wait for their turn to speak and/or to be called on (Belcher, 1999). Survey and ethnographic research suggests that these struggles with speaking come from several different sources, including students' own insecurities about their language abilities, cultural differences and inhibitions, and the (less than optimal) ways in which some classroom discussions are facilitated (Ferris, 1998; Ferris & Tagg, 1996a; Mason, 1994). The good news is that international students who persevere often become more confident and fluent during their months and years in the United States, and their oral/aural proficiency begins to catch up with the "eye" learning they have done in their home countries.

"Ear" Learners' Oral Skills

As previously noted, late- and early-arriving resident students tend to have stronger oral skills than do international students (Goen et al., 2002; Muchisky & Tangren, 1999), with the exception of newly arrived immigrants who face the same challenges as international students but perhaps without the same amount of L1 proficiency and prior L2 instruction. In fact, it is one of the defining characteristics of early-arriving students (at least some of them) that they appear to be so fluent (sometimes even speaking with no discernable non-native accent) and so comfortable in the classroom that their instructors are unaware of their second language status until they receive a piece of writing from these students. Having received all or most of their education in American schools, they are accustomed to the informal, inter-active nature of many American classrooms and are less likely to be confused or made anxious by it.

Late-arriving resident students beyond their first year or two in the United States will also be relatively comfortable with listening and speaking in the classroom, but they will not be as proficient as the early arrivals, whose exposure to the language, culture, and educational environment began at a younger age and has spanned a longer period of time. The strong listening/speaking skills of the "ear" learners at the college/university level offer both advantages and disadvantages. The major advantage, of course, is that these students can for the most part follow what is happening in their classes and interact comfortably with classmates and instructors if they have questions or need assistance. Reid (2006a, pp. 13–14) provides a helpful summary of "the strengths of ear learners" who typically

1. have relatively developed English oral fluency
2. have highly developed listening skills, even for the more formal English of television and the public schools
3. use phrasal verbs and idioms with ease
4. understand reduced forms (e.g., *gonna wanna go*) effortlessly
5. speak in highly complex sentence structures naturally, without difficulty

6. understand what's hot and what's not: the slang, the body language, the pop music, the behaviors, the humor, and the "cool" clothes of the diverse students in the schools they attend

7. have some familiarity with the U.S. educational system, some "academic literacy," if only as more observers than participants

8. recognize and understand classroom behaviors such as group work, conversational turn-taking, and student input during classroom discussions

9. have had experience with

    a. the processes of registration and changing classes

    b. writing classroom conventions like pre-writing forms, face-to-face response to the writing of peers, and the overall organization of paragraphs and essays

    c. the use of computers in academic writing

    d. the use of U.S.-published textbooks

The potential problem, however, is that "ear" learners' relative oral/aural proficiency may lull the instructor (and students themselves) into thinking that certain students have stronger academic language skills than they in fact possess, allowing them to overlook gaps these students may have in literacy abilities, vocabulary, and grammar knowledge (see the discussion of the "invisible middle" student group in Chapter 5). Further, Reid notes that "the informal conversational English of "ear" learners is the foundation of many of their academic difficulties" (2006a, p. 15). The characteristics of "ear"-learner speech include short phrases and questions, heavy use of personal pronouns and present tense, informal pronunciation including reduced forms (*gonna*), and a limited vocabulary range (Reid, 2006a). In short, despite the fact that "ear" learners "have substantial success in communicating orally, and they know some things about the culture of U.S. schools," they "have faced various levels of failure in their academic experiences" (Reid, 2006a, pp. 14–15).

Specific Language Skills: Reading

Reading in general is a complex process involving the interaction of a reader's background knowledge (of language, content, and text structure) and the elements contained in a specific text (Birch, 2007; Grabe & Stoller, 2002; Hedgcock & Ferris, 2009; Hudson, 2007; Koda, 2004; Seymour & Walsh, 2006). Children learning to read in their L1 have the advantage of years of exposure to oral language acquisition that have helped them to develop a vocabulary of thousands of words, to master the phonological system, and to have strongly developed intuitions about the morphology and syntax of their first language. L1 college students who have always been educated in their L1 have 12 or more years of literacy experience and exposure in that language. In contrast, L2 readers started later in acquiring the target language, overall have less acquired knowledge of it, and have had less experience with and exposure to texts in the L2.

As previously shown in this chapter, the academic literacy demands of upper-secondary and post-secondary education are challenging, and even many L1 students are not adequately prepared to meet them and require remedial coursework in reading and/or writing when they begin college. These expectations are even more daunting for L2 readers, who do not have a linguistic foundation equivalent to that of their L1 peers, who may never have read much at all in the L2, and whose prior L2 education may not have adequately helped them to develop basic academic reading skills and strategies. Figure 2.3 provides one basic template of the types of reading skills needed to succeed in college-level reading.

For a variety of educational and sociocultural reasons, nearly all L2 students struggle with college-level reading tasks at two foundational levels: (1) the amount of unknown or unfamiliar vocabulary in academic texts, which may include general vocabulary, general academic vocabulary, and discipline-specific vocabulary; and (2) the amount of reading required, which is often far beyond their prior educational experiences in any language, but especially in L2.

Because international students are fully literate in L1 and have had formal instruction in L2, they have transferable reading skills and experience as well as a

---

FIGURE 2.3
Required Academic Reading Skills

- Analyze features & rhetorical devices in texts
- Analyze different types of "public documents" (e.g., speeches, debates, policy statements)
- Check & utilize facts from consumer, workplace, and public documents
- Analyze new words in reading materials
- Interpret new words (or new meanings of words or phrases) accurately
- Respond to tone & connotation
- Analyze how meaning is conveyed through organizational patterns
- Analyze how meaning is conveyed through syntax and word choice
- Use "systematic strategies" to record and organize information
- Analyze style (irony, mood, tone, etc.)
- Draw inferences & conclusions
- Write summaries of reading materials
- Understand significant ideas in texts
- Use textual evidence to support interpretations
- Analyze author's assumptions and beliefs
- Critique validity of arguments
- Synthesize/connect ideas from various sources

Source: Adapted from California State University (CSU) Expository Reading and Writing Task Force, 2008.

solid foundation in the grammar and vocabulary of the L2 to bring to L2 academic reading. However, while L1 literacy skills may have positive transfer effects on L2 reading (Cummins, 1979), if the L1 is typologically distant from the L2 with regard to writing systems, morphology, syntax, common text structures, and vocabulary, L1 knowledge may also cause cross-linguistic interference in L2 reading (Birch, 2007; Koda, 2004). International students may also have limited experience with reading extensively in L2 and may never have read more than a page or two at a time in English (Robb, 2001; Spack, 1997, 2004), so they will need encouragement and opportunities to read extensively in order to build speed and fluency in the L2. Finally, because international students have limited familiarity with the L2 culture, certain aspects of texts and tasks may be unfamiliar to them.

Late-arriving residents may or may not be fully literate in L1, depending on their educational backgrounds and the circumstances of their immigration. Also, because they have only been acquiring English for a few years and in most cases their L2 was developed through "ear learning," a strong foundation in the L2 cannot be assumed, either. In short, they have "the worst of both worlds"—neither the strong L1 literacy foundation possessed by international students nor the extensive naturalistic L2 acquisition opportunities experienced by early-arriving students. As a result, they may struggle with academic reading at the college level on a variety of levels, possessing neither literacy nor language skills adequate for the task.

Early-arriving students may also struggle with academic reading in college, but for different reasons. Most are not literate in L1, so they do not have fully developed literacy skills to transfer to L2 reading. In many ways their acquired knowledge of the L2, which began developing at an early age and has progressed over many years, parallels that of native English speakers. Nonetheless, relative to monolingual English speakers, they had a later start in English, and this fact may have affected their educational pathways from the beginning, as noted in Chapter 1. That said, a strong L2 oral language foundation is very facilitative for L2 reading, so early-arriving students have definite advantages over other late-arriving "ear" learners and even in some ways over international students. Their strong oral and sociocultural foundation will help them to approach L2 texts more confidently (because their general vocabulary knowledge is strong and they have advanced intuitions about the morphology and syntax of the L2) and to understand classroom discussions and lectures that may provide background information helpful for reading comprehension. However, they likely will need instruction and practice in the types of intensive reading skills outlined in Figure 2.3.

Specific Language Skills: Writing

For most post-secondary instructors, whether in English composition/ESL or across the disciplines, writing is the area in which they feel students in general and L2 students in particular have the most difficulty in meeting academic standards (Adamson, 1993; Hartman & Tarone, 1999). After all, it can be difficult for professors to assess students' difficulties with listening and reading, receptive skills that can only be measured through students' performance on examinations, homework assignments, papers, and projects, or perhaps through contributions in in-class discussion or on an online class discussion board. In contrast, instructors in many disciplines tend to measure students' progress in the course primarily through written tasks, so if the writing itself is logically unclear and/or replete with problems with language and organization, professors will not only be confused but frustrated. At minimum, they expect that as students transition to college, they will have acquired, if not mastered, writing skills such as the ones listed in Figure 2.4.

Second Language Writers: Generalizations from Previous Research

L2 Writers: Three Observations

There are important distinctions across L2 student writer audiences, and these differences have important implications for practice. However, there are certain aspects of "being an L2 writer" that are somewhat universal. First of all, *a second language student writer is simultaneously grappling with language acquisition and writing proficiency development.* In contrast, while monolingual L1 student writers also have a great deal to learn about writing and often struggle with writing successfully, for the most part they at least have a fully developed range of linguistic tools at their disposal as they write. As for L2 writers, when the length of time it takes to acquire academic language proficiency in a second language is considered—perhaps seven years or longer (Collier, 1987, 1989; Cummins, 1979)—the task of the college-level L2 writer is daunting indeed.

FIGURE 2.4
Required Academic Writing Skills

- Synthesize ideas from several sources; make connections and "identify complexities and disparities" among sources
- Integrate quotations & citations into own text
- Use a style sheet appropriately for citations, notes, and bibliographies
- Use strategies to organize and record information from non-traditional sources (oral histories, interviews, websites, etc.)
- Analyze purpose, audience, and form for various assignment types
- Write well-focused texts that demonstrate purpose and audience awareness
- Structure ideas and arguments and support them effectively
- Revise writing to improve logic, organization, word choice, and tone
- Correctly use clauses, phrases, sentences, consistent verb tenses, grammar, usage, and diction
- Produce accurate texts that conform to manuscript specifications

---

Source: Adapted from CSU Expository Reading and Writing Task Force, 2008.

A second and related observation is that *second language student writers have not had adequate exposure to the English language, particularly written English.* Developing a second language vocabulary sufficient for college-level reading and writing is an enormous task of great complexity, particularly for L2 acquirers of English, which has an unusually large and varied lexicon (Birch, 2007; Folse, 2004, 2008; Conrad, 2008; Grabe & Stoller, 2002; Hedgcock & Ferris, 2009; Hinkel, 2004; Hudson, 2007; Koda, 2004; Nation, 2001; Scarcella, 2003). English L2 writers may struggle with choosing the appropriate word (as to meaning) or word form, with collocations (e.g., *tell a story* but not *say a story* or *speak a story*), with register (e.g., not understanding that conversational markers such as *Well, . . .* or slang usage such as *that really sucked* are usually inappropriate in college writing), and using vocabulary to produce variety or an elevated, sophisticated, mature writing style (Folse, 2008). The challenge of acquiring academic L2 vocabulary is so formidable, in fact, that it most likely cannot be accomplished without extensive reading in the L2 (Coxhead, 2000, 2006; Day & Bamford, 1998; Ferris & Hedgcock, 2005; Hedgcock & Ferris, 2009; Krashen, 2004; Koda, 2004; Seymour & Walsh, 2006). Similarly, many rules and facets of English grammar and vocabulary are so idiosyncratic and fundamentally unteachable (preposition/particle usage being one glaring example) that only extended and varied exposure to the patterns of the language, especially through reading, will facilitate their acquisition. This latter point is significant because many of the language errors made by L2 writers fall into the "untreatable" category (Ferris, 1999, 2002, 2006; Ferris & Roberts, 2001), meaning that no amount of classroom grammar instruction, no matter how well executed, will succeed in helping students to completely avoid those particular errors in their writing.

A third generalization about college-level second language writers is that *their prior experience with academic L2 writing is likely to be limited.* In the case of international students and late-arriving residents, if they have had previous classroom instruction in English in their home countries, it most typically emphasized grammar and vocabulary rather than extended composition. In many contexts, there was also relatively little writing instruction even in the L1, as in the story of Spack's "Yuko" (1997/2004), but even if there was some prior L1 writing development (see Kobayashi & Rinnert, 2002), for the reasons already outlined, it is more challenging for most students to write in a second language than in the first. As for resident students who graduated from U.S. high schools, many spent their years of secondary English in ESL classes, which also offered limited opportunities to develop academic writing skills (Bosher & Rowekamp, 1998; Harklau, 1994; Hartman & Tarone, 1999; Roberge, 2002). Although there are exceptional students and exemplary teachers and programs at the secondary level for L2 writers (e.g., Lay et al., 1999), for most L2 writers at the college level, the generalization holds that they have had neither adequate prior writing instruction nor enough practice in writing in the L2.[2]

Research on L2 Writers' Texts

Beyond these general observations, several researchers and reviewers over the years have summarized features and characteristics of English L2 writers' texts. For example, Silva (1993) reviewed 73 previous studies comparing L1 and L2 writing, finding that

> In general, L2 writers' texts were less fluent (fewer words), less accurate (more errors), and less effective (lower holistic scores). At the discourse level, their texts often exhibited distinct patterns of exposition, argumentation, and narration; their responses to two particular types of academic writing tasks—answering essay exam questions and using background reading texts—were different and less effective. Their orientation of readers was deemed less appropriate and acceptable. In terms of lower level linguistic concerns, L2 writers' texts were stylistically distinct and simpler in structure. Their sentences included more but shorter T-units, fewer but longer clauses, more coordination, less subordination, less noun modification, and less passivization. They evidenced distinct patterns in the use of cohesive devices, especially conjunctive (more) and lexical (fewer) ties, and exhibited less lexical control, variety, and sophistication overall. (p. 668)

Though Silva is careful to qualify his findings by discussing inconsistencies in design and lack of available information in some studies about subject characteristics, most experienced teachers of L2 writers would agree that, overall, Silva's summary is an accurate one. More recent corpus-based studies by Hinkel (2002), Hyland (2002), and Reynolds (2005) provided additional support for the claims made by Silva.

Writing Issues across the Three L2 Student Audiences

Writing Skills: International Students

With regard to L2 academic writing, international students have both advantages and disadvantages compared with the other two student populations. Their strong L1 academic literacy background as well as a foundation in L2 learning that emphasized grammar and vocabulary learning—both of which are helpful building blocks for successful L2 writing—have been noted. On the other hand, they may not have had much writing experience in L1 or L2, so they may have fluency and composing challenges, and they may not have been exposed to writing process approach techniques (pre-writing, multiple drafting, peer and expert feedback, revision, and editing) that are common to American composition instruction at the college level and increasingly in K–12 settings (Kroll, 1990a; Reid, 1998/2006b, 2006a). They may also be influenced by contrasting intercultural rhetoric patterns between L1 and L2 discourse, which could affect their approaches to text structure, to providing background information and appropriate detail for an audience, or taking a clear position or expressing an opinion (Connor, 1996, 2003; Ferris & Hedgcock, 2005; Kaplan, 1966). As noted by Leki (1992): "Sometimes ESL writing appears odd not because of errors, but because it gives the native reader an ineffable sense that the writing misses the point. . . . the rules for presenting ideas and strategies for explaining and defending them . . . are not completely interchangeable across cultures" (p. 88).

John's Text

The text excerpt that follows was written by the international student, John, whom we met in Chapter 1. It is part of a complete essay written for his ESL basic writing course two levels below the college freshman composition course. The topic was "lying" (whether it is harmful or acceptable), and it was based on an assigned class reading called "White Lies." (Thaler, the author, is referenced in this paragraph.)

> First of all, if people lie once, they might lie again **mostly** likely because they need another lie to cover the whole story. As a result, they have to lie all the time. I cannot **image that** what the relationship would be if the relationship is **maintain** by lying. Once a relationship is broken, it is very hard to maintain the relationship that it was supposed to be. It's like a broken window that can be replaced but it cannot be fixed. For example, I didn't expect **that I was involved** in a car accident on last Friday, but it **was happened**. I was thinking **that** lying to my mother that I didn't have a car accident so that she **won't** worry about me. But I am an honest person. I **can** lie to my **relative including** my mother, so I **decide tell me** mother the truth instead of lying to my mother that I didn't have a car accident**, I perfect telling** the truth **with** my mother at **a** right time and place so that she can relax and listen to **me how** the accident occurred. As a result, my mom **understands** that I **am** all right after the accident occurred so that she **doesn't** worry about me. Even though Thaler claims that lying can protect an intimate relationship, it **doesn't** work in my **cases.**

John's text is moderately to generally comprehensible, it stays on topic, and it shows a basic understanding of "typical" paragraph structure: topic sentence, support with an example, and summary sentence. He makes the rhetorical move

in the final sentence of arguing against the author, *Even though Thaler claims.*
. . . However, even within that general paragraph "formula," there are problems
in execution. For instance, the story John relates does not support the proposition
in the topic sentence: That one lie leads to another. Rather, the example simply
illustrates a time when he was tempted to keep from his mother that he had been
in a car accident but chose not to because he is "an honest person." Similarly, the
final sentence suggests that he is overgeneralizing from his personal experience,
and thus, he does not truly counter Thaler's assertion that "lying can protect an
intimate relationship."

The even more noticeable aspects of John's text are his limitations and errors
(noted in **bold**) in language. John's word choice is repetitive and his sentence
structure is simple—and when he attempts more complex sentences, the syntax
and comprehensibility break down. He has errors in verb tense and form as he tells
his past tense anecdote, and he makes errors in word choice and form (*image* and
perfect). These are fairly typical ESL errors found in the writing of incipient bilinguals (Valdés, 1992/2006; see Chapter 1). Considering the problems in development
and argumentation together with the simple writing style and the errors, there is
virtually no chance that John will pass his writing course or the graduation writing
examination he is preparing for if he continues to write at this level.

It is important to note that many college-level international students do not
even write as competently as John does. The international student text provided
for illustration by Reid (1997; 1998/2006b, see p. 79) has many serious errors that
greatly interfere with its comprehensibility; these errors include the use of false
cognates (words that are similar in L1 and L2 but do not have identical meanings), L1 transfer (sentence structure that follows L1 grammar patterns rather than
English), and the misuse of idiomatic expressions.

Writing Skills: Late-Arriving Resident Students

Late-arriving resident student writers will demonstrate writing problems that illustrate their late start in L2 acquisition as well as the fact they are "ear" learners who
have "picked up" the English language in natural settings rather than learning it
formally in a classroom. They are less likely to be well educated and literate in their
L1, so contrastive rhetoric issues may not be as salient for them as for international
students, but they also may not have had much composition instruction in English
prior to arriving at college.

Hector's Text

The next text excerpt was written by late-arriving immigrant subject, Hector, whom
we met in Chapter 1. Hector wrote this summary paper for his freshman English
(mainstream) class, which was studying *Huckleberry Finn.*

> Huckleberry and his friends started their travel **at** New Orleans where the Mississippi river starts in the south and went all the way north. Their objective was to **rich** to Cairo, the first town where Jim would be free. **In** their way the found all kind of adventures, **among** the way Huckleberry questions himself whether to **turn** Jim to his owner Ms Watson or not, but he decides he won't. One foggy day when they are almost in Cairo, they decide to stop because they think they may have passed Cairo without seeing it. Then they get their boat stolen.

Hector demonstrates fairly competent summary skills. For example, in the third sentence, he says that Huckleberry and his friends have many adventures on their way to Cairo and that he struggles all along with helping Jim escape from his owner—good summary statements without extraneous detail. He accurately uses complex sentence structure, including instances of coordination and subordination, but his vocabulary is quite simple.

Hector's most frequent error in the sample involves the inappropriate shifting of verb tenses from past to present tense; while the "literary present tense" is acceptable in the summary of a story, Hector needs to be consistent in using either present or past tense throughout the summary. However, many L1 student writers struggle with tense-shifting in narration, so this issue cannot necessarily be attributed to Hector's L2 status. On the contrary, he demonstrates in the first several sentences that he is aware of English past tense forms and can use them appropriately. Hector makes two preposition errors (*at New Orleans; in their way*) that are fairly typical for L2 writers from all language backgrounds and several lexical errors (*rich* instead of *reach,* which is likely an interference error from his L1, Spanish; *among* instead of *along,* which may simply be a typing or spelling error; and *turn* instead of *return,* which may be an attempted use of the idiom *to turn someone in*). In short, while Hector's writing is not bad for a recently arrived immigrant student, it would readily be identified as coming from an L2 writer due to the ESL-type errors and the limited range of vocabulary used. Again, some late-arriving resident student writers at the college level are much less proficient than Hector, who, as discussed in Chapter 1, had a fairly complete L1 education and years of classroom English study in his home country of Mexico. (For other examples, see Reid's sample text, 1998/2006b, p. 77; see also sample texts from *California Pathways* [Browning et al., 2000]).

Writing Skills: Early-Arriving Resident Students

Early arrivals who have had all or most of their schooling in the L2 have some advantages over both international and late-arriving resident student writers. As previously mentioned, their acquired sense of the language is more developed than that of student writers who have not been in the United States as long, so they have better intuitions about phrase and sentence structure, idiomatic expressions and collocations, and a well developed general vocabulary. Since very few have extensive L1 literacy experience, they do not have contrastive or intercultural rhetoric issues to grapple with, and they have likely had some prior instruction on paragraph and essay structure and elements of the composing process (Kroll, 1990a). They also have a well-developed awareness of the L2 culture, which may help them to approach topics, reading texts, and tasks with more confidence than students with less cultural background knowledge.

However, early arrivals face challenges that are somewhat unique to their particular circumstances. As "ear" learners, they may have picked up English from other functional bilinguals and/or monolinguals who speak a non-standard variety, and some of these patterns may need to be re-analyzed and adapted for the purposes of producing standard academic written English. Also, because their educational pathways may not have led to adequate development of academic literacy, their writing may be overly conversational and informal, reflecting inappropriate selection of register (*it is imperative to hang around with a large number of friends*) or inaccurate "translation" from spoken to written English (*He should of left early*) (examples adapted from Reid, 2006a, p. 20). Early-arriving resident students' writing may also include phonetic spellings of words or phrases they have heard but not read (e.g., *firstable* instead of *first of all*). Finally, Generation 1.5 writers may make errors more characteristic of less proficient ("basic" or "remedial") L1 writers than of other ESL writers, e.g., *your* instead of *you're* (Reid, 2006a, p. 21).

Luciana's Text

To illustrate this point, let us consider a text excerpt from Luciana, our early-arriving case study subject from Chapter 1, from an essay written for her basic writing course (the native-speaker course one semester below college-level):

> In this particular quote Anzaldua mentions how hard it is sometimes for Mexicans to become accustomed to a new environment and culture. Many **persons loose** job opportunities **for** not being able to acculturate. A way of acculturating could be speaking Standard English because that is what society expects from any person **that** wishes to work. I know this **for fact** because my parents could not get a well-paid job because they did not **spoke** English. They had to work in the fields **because is** the only place **were** language is **not require-ment**. I think **that type of situations** happens to **persons** of all cultures, not only Mexicans, **which** have immigrated to the United States without even having **notion of** English.

Luciana's paragraph is clearly focused and well structured, moving from a paraphrase of a previous quotation to a specific point with a relevant example from personal experience to a closing sentence that not only summarizes the example but generalizes it to other people. Her vocabulary is more academic than that of Hector and John. Her sentence structure is complex and for the most part accurate, with the first and last sentences of the paragraph serving as good examples. Her errors, shown in bold type, are, as expected, a mixture of typical ESL errors and basic writer errors. For example, the sentence *They had to work in the fields because is* . . . is clearly an example of Spanish L1 interference; other possible examples of this are *for not being able to acculturate* and *without even having notion of English* (*notion* in English and *noción* in Spanish are near-cognates). In contrast, *loose* instead of *lose*, *persons* instead of *people*, and the inappropriate use of the relative pronouns *which/that* to refer to people are errors also made by less-skilled L1 writers. Luciana's particular background of coming from a transnational family likely has resulted in the Spanish L1 interference, as she not only grew up in a Spanish-speaking home with parents who did not speak English but spent significant amounts of time in Mexico and had part of her schooling there. Other early-arriving resident students whose profiles fall into the other categories outlined by Roberge (2002) and Reid (2006a) would demonstrate different needs in their texts. In short, while all L2 writers share some common struggles, there is tremendous variation across individual students that can at least in part be traced to their differing backgrounds.

This chapter looked closely at the requirements of what is called "Academic English" and discussed ways in which the three student audiences defined in Chapter 1 are more or less prepared, depending on their backgrounds, to meet those expectations. The degree of L1 academic literacy and L2 acquisition affects the different groups in various ways—but for all three groups, the acquisition and production of academic English that is adequate for post-secondary study is a tremendous challenge. Parts 2 and 3 address the ways in which programs and individual instructors can discern and attempt to meet the diverse needs of these different student audiences.

QUESTIONS FOR REFLECTION AND DISCUSSION

1. The opening section of this chapter outlines the various dimensions of academic language and literacy that *all* students, regardless of background, need for success in post-secondary contexts. Which of these (if any) were new ideas for you? Can you think of any that are missing?

2. This chapter implies that L2 students in general are at a fundamental disadvantage, compared with monolingual L1 peers, in coping with the demands of academic language/literacy at the college or university level. What arguments and information are presented that might support this generalization? What problems or dangers might exist in accepting it uncritically?

3. This chapter suggests that it is more important to focus on academic literacy (reading/writing) than on other language skills (listening/speaking) for student success in higher education. Do you agree or disagree with this perspective, and why?

4. Look again at the analyses of the student text excerpts by John, Hector, and Luciana. Would you add anything to these analyses or change anything about them? If you were teaching or tutoring one of these students, what do you think this student most needs to work on, and how would you approach the task? If you are in contact with any L2 writers, see if you can obtain a text sample, and analyze it, looking specifically at some of the text features mentioned in this section. What can you add to the observations made in this chapter?

5. This chapter fundamentally makes three points: (1) Academic language and literacy skills are difficult to master and become more so at post-secondary levels; (2) L2 students face a number of challenges as they grapple with academic demands; and (3) different L2 "audiences" have distinct characteristics and needs due to their varying educational pathways. What are the possible implications of these issues for program development, course design, and classroom instruction? Jot down some ideas, being as specific as you can. Revisit these notes after you have read Part 2 (Chapter 3–5) of this book.

CHAPTER ENDNOTES

[1] A recent study of community college students in California found that while more students than ever before are attempting college, only about 25 percent meet specific benchmarks—completing a certificate, associate's degree, or transferring to a four-year school—within six years, and the numbers are even lower for minority students (Pope, 2007).

[2] While some advocates of extensive reading would dismiss writing "practice" as a significant variable in the development of proficient writing skills (Krashen, 2004), others would argue that the thinking and decision-making processes that go into the production of a text provide valuable experience that builds confidence and competence for future writing tasks (see Ferris & Hedgcock, 2005)—in other words, while exposure to the second language, especially L2 text, is critical for building writing skills, we also learn to write by *writing*.

PART 2
Implications

Chapter 3

Different Student Audiences and Programmatic Issues

Although classroom issues are important, such narrow focus on the classroom is problematic because instruction is always situated in and shaped by larger institutional contexts.

—Matsuda, Ortmeier-Hooper, & You, 2006, p. vii

PART 1: FOUNDATIONS GAVE ATTENTION TO *definition* (Chapter 1) of the three L2 student audiences (**international, late-arriving** resident, and **early-arriving** resident students) and *description* of their characteristics and needs, focusing particularly in Chapter 2 on the academic language demands that all students face, regardless of linguistic or cultural origins, and on ways in which those expectations pose particular challenges for the various groups of L2 students we have defined. Part 2: Implications focuses on practical implications of understanding the student audiences, moving from general issues (curriculum, placement, assessment, and teacher preparation) to more specific ones (course design and classroom instruction). As will be shown, the literature on these topics paints a complex picture, and there is (as noted by Matsuda, 2008, p. 171) "no one-size-fits-all" approach. However, we can at least outline the issues, discuss the possibilities, and begin to articulate some principles that administrators and curriculum designers can adapt for use in their own context and programs.

Chapter 3 examines several related questions. First, as to curriculum and placement, *in what types of courses will L2 students best be served?* At the four-year college/university level, this question pertains mainly to the composition/reading/literacy tracks or course options available; in two-year colleges, students' choices often extend also to listening/speaking or grammar courses. Other placement questions include *how* L2 students are identified and placed and *who* should make those decisions. With regard to assessment, program-wide considerations include entrance/placement examinations for freshman courses, exit examinations (or alternative assessments) for specific course levels, and writing proficiency requirements for graduation. Finally, once courses have been designed and students have been placed in them, *who should teach these students, and how should those instructors*

FIGURE 3.1

Program Design: Issues & Questions

Issue	Questions
Curriculum	• Should college-level L2 students be in ESL or mainstream courses? • Should underprepared L2 students be in remedial ESL courses or in L1 basic writing courses (if such courses are offered)? • Should different L2 audiences be in ESL courses separate from one another?
Placement	• How can L2 students be identified? • By what mechanisms should they be placed into appropriate courses? • Should placements be compulsory or voluntary? • Who should make placement decisions?
Assessment	• What types of assessments are appropriate and fair for L2 students (especially L2 writers)? • Should L2 writers be assessed only by L2 specialists?
Teacher preparation	• What preparation is needed for teachers of L2 courses? • How can instructors in mainstream composition courses and peer tutors in writing/learners centers be prepared to work with L2 writers?

be prepared? In discussing the teacher preparation issue, we will consider not only ESL or composition classes but also support systems such as writing centers and adjunct courses. Figure 3.1 outlines the subtopics and questions to be examined.

Curriculum and Placement

Curricular Questions: ESL or Mainstream Courses?

Most two- and four-year colleges and universities have some sort of first-year English language/literacy requirement for their students. First pioneered by Harvard University in 1885 in the United States, this requirement is most typically realized as "freshman composition," though there is now a wide range of labels and names given to such courses (Connors, 1993). In some institutions, students are only required to take a one-term course, and in many others, they must take a full year of English reading/writing courses as part of their general education requirements for graduation. It is also quite typical for institutions to have some sort of entrance or placement examination (e.g., the University of California Subject A exam discussed in Frodesen & Starna, 1999, and Holten, 2002; see also Costino & Hyon, 2007, for discussion of a parallel mechanism at the California State University) for these first-year courses. A substantial percentage of entering students fail or receive a low score on this examination, which necessitates their placement in pre–collegiate level courses variously known as remedial or basic or developmental writing classes (Parsad & Lewis, 2000).

As discussed by Matsuda (2006b), as the number of international students attending U.S. colleges and universities increased following World War II, universities began considering whether these ESL students belonged in mainstream freshman composition courses or in separate courses designed especially for them. With regard to these traditional ESL students (who later included the "first wave" of voluntary immigrants and refugees in the 1970s), there has been (and is to this day) a divergence of opinion about their placement in college-level writing courses. Many experts in composition studies have felt strongly that once L2 students reach college-level coursework, they should be mainstreamed in courses with their English-speaking peers, with no further accommodations (e.g., separate courses, specially trained teachers, specially designed materials or curriculum, different grading/assessment standards) for their language-learner status necessary or appropriate (e.g., Roy, 1988). Others have argued that writing programs have an ethical obligation (Conference on College Composition & Communication, 2001; Silva, 1997) to offer separate placement options for ESL students. Further, some mainstream composition teachers complain about having ESL writers in their classes or see their presence as a problem (Edlund, 2003; Frodesen & Starna, 1999; Matsuda, 2006b). To this day, both models (mainstreaming and separate ESL courses) exist in colleges and universities around the United States (Braine, 1996; Costino & Hyon, 2007). However, it is also fair to say that even where separate ESL offerings exist, there are also many L2 students who are mainstreamed, either by their own choice (even fueled by perceptions that mainstream courses/instructors will be easier for them) or by necessity (not enough ESL sections or program policies that place only traditional ESL students such as internationals in ESL-designated courses). Thus, it would be oversimplifying the case to suggest that L2 writers at U.S. colleges and universities are either all in ESL classes or all mainstreamed at their particular institutions.[1] For nuanced discussions of placement models for L2 writers, see Matsuda (2006a) and Silva (1994).

The issue of mainstreaming vs. segregating (Edlund, 2003, p. 363) ESL students in required composition courses becomes even more complex when resident students, especially early-arrivals, are considered. While it is relatively easy to identify international students, it is far less straightforward to determine whether permanent U.S. residents and naturalized or native-born U.S. citizens coming from U.S. high schools and/or transferring from local two-year colleges warrant "ESL treatment" (e.g., special placement examinations and courses). Most often, the issue of appropriate placement only surfaces when the students have already enrolled in mainstream college composition or basic writing courses and a teacher or administrator, looking at the student's biodata and/or writing sample, raises the question of whether the student is an English learner who needs specialized instruction.

Besides the practical issues of identification, there is the even more complicated matter of how we define *native* and *non-native* speakers in a society and educational system in which such boundaries are increasingly ill-defined and definitions are more elusive. As noted by Harklau, Siegal, & Losey, "the current division of labor among regular composition, basic or developmental composition, and ESL *tends to assume discrete populations of students can be distinguished as the clientele of each.* . . . [Generation 1.5 learners] present a fundamental challenge to program divisions" (1999, p. 11, emphasis added). Chiang and Schmida, reflecting on their student case study subjects at UC–Berkeley, point out that "our students do not neatly fit into clean-cut categories such as mainstream English speaker, ESL speaker, or bilingual students" (1999, p. 91). To summarize, the question is: Are these early-arriving U.S.-educated students *non-native speakers* because their parents are and because the first language they heard in the home was not English, or are they *native speakers* because all or most of their education was received in English and English is the only language in which they have ever functioned academically? There is room for debate at more general, abstract levels of the question—and a need for diverse responses and options when specific individual students or subgroups in various contexts are considered.

It might be assumed that in programs or departments where separate ESL courses are offered, the L2 writers would neatly divide into one of two groups: ESL classes for the traditional (international and late-arriving residents) students and mainstream classes for the early-arriving L2 students. In reality, however, while the international students do in fact typically end up in ESL classes (if available), the early- and late-arriving residents may also be found in ESL classes in increasing proportions (Costino & Hyon, 2007; Ferris, 1998; Goen et al., 2002; Muchisky & Tangren, 1999), while others at the same institutions enroll in mainstream classes (Costino & Hyon, 2007; Edlund, 2003; Matsuda & Silva, 1999; Ortmeier-Hooper, 2008). This latter group may be found in college-level (first-year or freshman) composition courses or basic/developmental writing courses, and they may enroll in those courses either from ignorance of the ESL options or by choice, as they do not self-identify as ESL students (Blanton, 1999; Chiang & Schmida, 1999; Costino & Hyon, 2007; Frodesen & Starna, 1999; Goen et al., 2002; Harklau, 2000; Holten, 2002; Matsuda, 2008; Ortmeier-Hooper, 2008). It is also important to note that in many college writing programs, the number of specialized or designated ESL/L2/multilingual sections available does not meet potential student demand. It is certainly fair to say in many cases that if L2 students in ESL and mainstream composition classes in the same department were compared as to their backgrounds and their writing abilities, there would be considerable overlap and debate over which student belonged where (see, e.g., Frodesen & Starna, 1999).

On the other hand, in contexts where separate ESL courses are not offered at the degree-granting baccalaureate level, there have been several different approaches to addressing the needs of L2 students who arrive in college with inadequate skills for the mainstream college-level composition course(s) (Braine, 1996). One common approach is to "outsource" the L2 students to separate language development programs, such as intensive language, community college, or adult education programs or to remedial non-credit on-campus programs (Atkinson & Ramanathan, 1995; Lay et al., 1999; Matsuda, 2006b; Wurr, 2004). These programs may help to provide the linguistic and academic foundation that students will need to succeed in their college/university studies. However, the problem for many students is that such remediation is almost never credit-bearing and places financial burdens on both international students (whose expensive stay in the host country is lengthened by these additional language course requirements) (Leki, 1992) and on resident L2 students (who often have substantial financial challenges and whose financial aid may be compromised by having to take courses that do not provide credit toward graduation) (Browning et al., 2000; Lay et al., 1999; Roberge, 2002; Wurr, 2004). Further, such language courses are not always similar philosophically and pedagogically to the mainstream programs for which they are preparing students (Atkinson & Ramanathan, 1995; Tarone & Hartman, 1999) and, especially in the case of intensive language programs, may not be designed with the needs of resident L2 students in mind (Blanton, 1999; Muchisky & Tangren, 1999; Wurr, 2004).

The other common approach to "remediating" ESL students in mainstream composition programs is to place them into basic writing courses primarily serving monolingual English speakers, the logic being that since their language/writing skills are not at the college level (at least in the judgment of those making such decisions), they belong in basic writing classes along with other students whose skills have similarly been judged inadequate. The problem, of course, is that the needs of L2 writers and the needs of L1 basic writers are not identical, and the educational paths that led to their placement in the basic writing course are likely quite different. Many scholars (both in ESL and basic writing camps) have questioned whether basic writing courses intended for native English speakers are the best place for any L2 student, whether international or resident (e.g., Benson, Deming, Denzer, & Valeri-Gold, 1992; Blanton, 1999; Braine, 1996; Matsuda, 2003a, 2008). Blanton (1999) notes that many basic writing instructors do not feel equipped to work with L2 students and characterizes such courses as "excessively form-centered, stigmatized, focused on the language problems of 'nonmainstream dialect speakers', and not focused enough on L2 issues" (pp. 126–127). While some might feel that Blanton's description is overly harsh, it is fair to note that L1 students in basic writing classes have a variety of special needs that may not be shared by recent arrivals (international and late-arriving resident students). Some of those L1 basic writers' needs may also apply to *some* early-arriving students, but others may have been highly successful high school students who arrive in college "deficient" only in second language acquisition (but without other academic problems).

So do basic L2 writers (i.e., those who are judged not ready for college-level writing courses) belong in non-credit ESL classes, or do they belong in L1 basic writing courses? It would seem that most or all L2 writers below the college level would be better off in specially designed ESL courses (ideally courses that provide credit toward graduation[2])—but again, the issue is complicated by the blurring distinctions between native and non-native speakers (Costino & Hyon, 2007). Take the case of Luciana, the early-arriving student introduced in Chapters 1–2, who was in fact enrolled in an L1 basic writing course even though an equivalent ESL course was available to her. Her writing (shown and discussed in Chapter 2) shows both ESL and basic writer characteristics, and her educational background is more similar to that of a typical L1 basic writer than that of a traditional ESL student such as an international student or newly arrived resident. Where would Luciana best be served? As further illustration, two multilingual interview subjects in Costino and Hyon's (2007) study who had taken mainstream basic writing courses and then gone on to mainstream first-year writing courses said that they were satisfied with their experiences in the basic writing courses and would not change anything if they could go back and make different decisions. On the other hand, the other interview subjects in the Costino and Hyon study, who had taken the ESL version of the basic writing course, also expressed satisfaction with their choices and experiences. This is to say that there is likely no one "best" answer for students such as Luciana.

Curricular Questions: Which ESL Course?

For institutions, departments, and programs that do offer a separate, equivalent track of ESL courses and for students enrolled in those programs (whether by choice or requirement), our understanding of the three L2 audiences raises further questions as to whether all L2 students, regardless of background, should be taught together in the same course(s). Over the past several decades, this issue has evolved and emerged in several different ways, depending on the context and demographic characteristics of the institution and students. For example, Muchisky and Tangren (1999) describe how their ESL program in Nebraska, which largely serves international students, has adapted to accommodate a small but growing number of resident L2 students. In many ESL programs around the United States, it is still the case that the focus of their program is on international students (Blanton, 1999), yet they are increasingly noticing the presence and impact of resident students in their classes. However, in other parts of the country, such as California and New York, the student audience in ESL programs has shifted dramatically in recent decades (Frodesen, 2002; Frodesen & Starna, 1999; Goen et al., 2002; Harklau, Siegal, & Losey, 1999; Holten, 2002), and resident students (both late- and early-arriving) now comprise the vast majority of the ESL population (e.g., Goen et al., 2002).

Matsuda (2008) rightly calls the idea that international and immigrant L2 students cannot be taught in the same classes a "myth," and further observes that ever-shifting populations and limited resources may make separate course options for different groups of L2 students impractical. Still, it is important to point out some of the problems and challenges of a "one-size-fits-all" approach to ESL curriculum design and program planning. First, as discussed in Chapter 2, the different student audiences arrive at college with diverse needs. International students typically have strengths in formal language knowledge (L2 grammar and vocabulary) and effective academic/literacy skills and strategies developed in the L1, but they often lack fluency, confidence and experience, and cultural knowledge (Blanton, 1999; Costino & Hyon, 2007; Edlund, 2003; Kroll, 1990a; Leki, 1992; Reid, 1998/2006b). Late-arriving and early-arriving resident students, on the other hand, typically possess strong listening and speaking skills and are well acclimated culturally but often have weak formal language skills and inadequate literacy abilities (Reid, 1998/2006b; Roberge, 2002; Wurr, 2004). Second, the students have drastically different life experiences. Third, and perhaps most important, L2 students are often uncomfortable being placed into classes with other ESL students who are not like them. This tension is most often expressed in terms of the "insult' that early-arriving resident students feel at being labeled "ESL" in college even though they have lived most or all of their lives in the L2-dominant country (e.g., Blanton, 1999; Chiang & Schmida, 1999; Costino & Hyon, 2007; Frodesen & Starna, 1999; Goen et al., 2002; Leki, 1999; Matsuda, 2008; Ortmeier-Hooper, 2008). In contrast, in contexts where international students have become the minority group in ESL programs (e.g., Goen et al., 2002), it is possible that their needs as relative newcomers can also be overlooked as teachers aim their instruction at the majority resident student audience. Thus, where feasible, it could be valuable to offer separate ESL courses (or sections of courses) tailored for different audiences (see Chapter 6).

To summarize, it may seem better to have all or many of the L2 students together in the same ESL program than to have some or all of them mainstreamed into L1 programs. After all, despite their differences, they have substantial similarities (see Chapter 2), and surely they would be better off in classes designed and taught by program developers and instructors who are aware of L2 acquisition processes and equipped to meet L2 students' needs. However, the complexity and the blurred boundaries within and between the various student audiences argues against such an "easy" conclusion and in favor of a broad range of curricular options, improved placement mechanisms, more enlightened course designs, and better-equipped instructors (in ESL, mainstream composition, and writing centers) (Blanton, 1999; Costino & Hyon, 2007; Harklau, Siegal, & Losey, 1999; Wolfe-Quintero & Segade, 1999; Wurr, 2004).

Placement Issues: Identification of L2 Students

A matter closely related to that of curricular options is that of placement: *How* should second language students be placed and *who* should make those decisions? Under the *how* question fall several connected issues, including **identification** of L2 students in various audiences, **mechanisms** for placing them once they are identified, and whether such placements are **mandatory or voluntary.** As to the first issue, identification, we have already noted that while it is a fairly easy matter to identify and contact international students (through their visa status and the international students' office), it is more complex to ascertain which students are U.S.-resident late- or early-arrivals who might benefit from L2 placement. As permanent residents or naturalized or native-born U.S. citizens, their student identification numbers will not be clues to their status, nor, given the cultural and ethnic diversity in the United States, can surnames be a reliable indicator of L2 status.

As previously noted, many institutions require a placement examination for all incoming freshmen to see whether they are in fact prepared for first-year composition courses; those who score below a certain threshold are placed into remedial/ basic writing sequences. Some colleges and universities now ask students taking this examination to fill out a language background survey, and this information can help schools to identify possible candidates for multilingual/ESL/L2 class placements (if they are available). However, this is not a perfect solution for several reasons. For one, in many contexts, students enter universities as transfer students, not freshmen, having taken some coursework at community colleges, and do not take the placement examination. If they transfer with remaining English requirements (e.g., first- or second-year composition, graduation writing assessments, or upper-division writing courses) to fulfill, it can be difficult to find them and let them know of L2 course options that might be open to them. Second, the types of labels and questions that might be found on language background surveys can themselves be problematic for students with shifting linguistic and cultural identities. In a recent study at a California State University campus, Costino and Hyon (2007) found that nine multilingual students whom they interviewed had varying interpretations of and comfort levels with terms such as *bilingual, multilingual, ESL,* and so forth. Some of their subjects' perceptions changed once the interviewers defined the labels more precisely, but such explanation would not be possible when students are filling out a survey during a large-scale placement examination. In other words, students who might benefit from multilingual placement options might be "missed" by such surveys.[3]

Besides residency/visa status and student responses on language background surveys, a third way students can be targeted for possible L2 placement is self-identification. If students become aware through advising or publicity that there are multilingual options open to them, they may initiate the process of ESL placement. For instance, at the California State University campus where I previously taught, students with a multilingual designation were given additional time on the junior-level writing proficiency examination (WPE) required for graduation, and these examinations were read separately by ESL-trained readers. In order to receive the "ESL administration" of the WPE, students had to voluntarily take the in-house ESL placement exam and take their test scores to the WPE office to certify that they were eligible for the extra time and separate reading of their WPE. In other words, it was to their benefit to voluntarily self-identify as multilingual, and once they were in the system, they could be contacted for advising and apprised of their options.[4] This is especially important, as noted, in a context where many students arrive as junior transfers and there are few other mechanisms to identify them.

Placement Issues: Mechanisms

Once L2 students have been identified through one or more of these various channels, there are several basic options for placing them into appropriate courses (e.g., mainstream or multilingual; different levels of an ESL program). In addition to large-scale placement mechanisms such as the Subject A examination (now known as the Academic Writing Proficiency Examination or AWPE) at the University of California, the English Placement Test at the California State University, and equivalent versions in other universities or systems, more finely tuned ESL placement tests can be administered. Many institutions choose to develop their own placement test, which may include subsections for reading and listening comprehension, grammar, a short essay, and perhaps an oral interview. While such placement tests are more typically used to determine which ESL course level would be most appropriate for students, as populations have become more diverse, they are also used to identify which multilingual students are not ESL, or functional bilinguals (Frodesen & Starna, 1999; Valdés, 1992/2006) who might be better served in mainstream courses.

As already noted, an alternative or complementary type of placement mechanism can be information from students themselves about their language and educational backgrounds (Costino & Hyon, 2007; Frodesen, 2002; Frodesen & Starna, 1999; Holten, 2002; Reid, 1998/2006b). Such data can be gathered through surveys or questionnaires collected when the student takes an ESL placement test and/or through follow-up interviews if there is continued ambiguity about the student's status. Background information from students is likely to be used primarily to resolve the "mainstream vs. multilingual" question, rather than whether the student belongs in basic writing or first-year composition courses or in a particular level of the ESL program. In other words, as L2 populations become more diverse, it is important to consider various types of information, including test scores, oral and/ or written language production, and student background information, to determine the most appropriate course of action for individual students. The Appendix at the end of this chapter (page 74) shows a sample questionnaire and interview questions that have been used to examine students' language backgrounds. Finally, some programs have begun to work with student "directed self-placement" (Crusan, 2002, 2006), though self-placement alone has not yet achieved widespread recognition or acceptance.

A final placement mechanism used on a smaller scale within programs is the "reassignment" of students from a mainstream class to a multilingual one (or, less commonly, vice versa) during the first week or so of classes. Such reassignments are most typically initiated by classroom teachers who have collected diagnostic writing samples and perhaps other information from/about students and have spotted students who, in their judgment, would be better served in an ESL/multilingual course. In some instances, the L2 students were not even aware that a multilingual course equivalent was an option for them (Costino & Hyon, 2007, and the case of Luciana and several of her classmates). While transfers like this can be awkward, given how hectic the beginning of a term can be and the logistical issues involved in changing classes, some thoughtful planning can facilitate the process.

Placement Issues: Student Choice

A final issue with regard to the mechanics of placement, once L2 students have been identified and various placement instruments have been utilized, is whether students will be *required* to follow placement recommendations or whether they are simply *advised* to do so. There are two separate questions to consider: (1) Can students opt into—or out of—multilingual or mainstream courses? (2) Must students enroll in the course indicated by their placement score? Philosophies and practices vary depending on the type of institution and students being served. In some settings, for instance, international students may have a hold placed on their registration and not be allowed to enroll in subject-matter classes until they have taken their ESL placement test and fulfilled any ESL course requirements. In other settings, if students have been placed into the multilingual track but decide they prefer to take mainstream courses, they may be strongly discouraged from doing so by ESL instructors or administrators who firmly believe that they have the students' best interests at heart and can better meet their specialized needs than the mainstream program can—or who simply do not want to lose the enrollments in the multilingual courses.

Conversely, L2 students who have either chosen to enroll in mainstream courses or who did so because they were unaware of multilingual equivalent options may find themselves being pressured by their mainstream instructor to transfer to a multilingual course because the instructor feels unwilling or unable to meet their needs. As to course-level issues, some community colleges have been constrained by legal decisions requiring them to allow students to self-place: While the colleges can require placement testing and advise students as to appropriate course options, students are allowed to place themselves higher or lower than their placement test indicates. These various approaches to the compulsory/voluntary placement continuum mean that in different institutions and contexts, a variety of scenarios may occur (or even co-occur):

- international students may be compelled into ESL course sequences, but other L2 students are not

- L2 students in multilingual courses who might do well in mainstream courses and might even prefer to take them are discouraged and even prevented from switching tracks

- L2 students who prefer to stay in mainstream courses are pressured and/or forced out of them into multilingual courses
- L2 students may be in the wrong instructional level for their language/literacy abilities

While it is obvious that placement problems can and do happen, as to the "choice" issue itself, many L2 writing experts would likely agree on the following two statements. First, where possible, *there should be equivalent and adequate multilingual course options available to L2 students* (Braine, 1996; CCCC, 2001; Silva, 1997).[5] Second, when multilingual tracks are offered, *L2 students should be able to choose whether to enroll in mainstream or multilingual writing/language sections* (Braine, 1996; CCCC, 2001; Costino & Hyon, 2007; Goen et al., 2002; Matsuda & Silva, 1999; Silva, 1997). This latter statement further implies that an adequate number of ESL/multilingual sections are offered and staffed to meet student demand, a condition that often is not satisfied in programs with scarce resources and conflicting needs.

Placement Issues: Who Decides?

Some aspects of the previous discussion have touched upon the *who* issue in place-ment: Who decides on the placement of these L2 students? Is it the mainstream composition program? The multilingual specialists? A university computer pro-gram? The students themselves? As noted, there are problems inherent in every option. Large-scale placement instruments designed for entire university systems may not be discriminating enough for a diverse and complex student audience. While many mainstream composition specialists are well informed about and sensi-tive to multilingual writing issues, others lack expertise and/or perspective or view students' needs from a differing philosophical stance (Atkinson & Ramanathan, 1995; Benson et al., 1992; Blanton, 1999; Braine, 1996; Costino & Hyon, 2007).

At one extreme, some composition specialists, along with other faculty across the disciplines, take the hard-line view that L2 students should be held to the same standards as monolingual native speakers and dismiss as "coddling" concerns raised by L2 experts about the rate and long-term success of second language acquisi-tion by adults and about the differences between L1 and L2 writers' texts (Collier, 1987, 1989; Silva, 1993; Valdés, 1992/2006). Even relatively minor L2 features in writing (i.e., the fossilized language of functional bilinguals discussed by Valdés, 1992/2006, and Frodesen & Starna, 1999) are judged harshly and the students themselves considered deficient. At the opposite extreme are instructors who feel that only students' content and writing processes are important, so the L2 features that might require or benefit from extra attention in a specialized writing course are irrelevant (and thus no justification for multilingual alternatives or placements). In between those extremes are instructors who do understand and make allowances for the fact the L2 acquisition takes time and that L2 texts will not look identical to those written by L1 students but who may not have the expertise or experience to judge whether a student's writing falls into the "incipient" or "functional" bilingual category (Frodesen & Starna, 1999; Valdés, 1992/2006).

This is not to say that mainstream writing instructors should have no role in placement decisions regarding L2 students. On the contrary, to the degree they can distinguish between the texts of L2 writers who are ready for and would benefit from mainstreaming and those who would thrive in multilingual instruction, their perspective can be very complementary to that of L2 specialists, who tend to be protective of the students and may not be objective enough to determine when some students would function well in mainstream courses. Ideally, in programs where there are diverse L2 student audiences and in which multilingual placement is an option, L1 and L2 writing specialists would work together to make placement recommendations appropriate for a complex student population (Costino & Hyon, 2007; Frodesen & Starna, 1999; Holten, 2002; Wurr, 2004). Finally, while students themselves probably need assistance from experts as to determining which option is most beneficial for them—that is, they should not be left entirely on their own to place themselves—they should not be forced into (or out of) multilingual options if they exist, and their opinions as to which track is best for them should be considered and respected (CCCC, 2001; Costino & Hyon, 2007; Harklau, 2000; Silva, 1997).

Assessment

The assessment of L2 students is another issue that has program-wide implications. Beyond placement testing are exit/entry assessments allowing students to move from one course level to the next and institutional graduation writing assessments. Issues or questions to consider include:

- What are/should be the *nature* of the assessments (e.g., timed vs. out-of-class or portfolio writing)?
- On what *skills* should students be assessed?
- Should there be *alternatives* to the assessment procedure, and if so, what should they be?
- *Who* should make the judgments?

What Type(s) of Assessments?

For large-scale assessment—that is, procedures that extend beyond individual teachers and their classrooms—the most pressing question tends to be whether students will be judged based on a single timed-writing examination or through some other means. For readily apparent practical reasons—relative ease and cost-efficiency of administration and scoring—timed writing assessed via holistic scoring is still the norm for most programs and institutions at colleges and universities when large numbers of student writers are being assessed (Weigle, 2002). Students can all come at one time and take a written essay examination that they complete within several hours; raters can be trained and complete their assessments within a day or a weekend; scoring procedures can be articulated, standardized, streamlined, and transparent. Though sometimes exceptions can be made (e.g., students with disabilities can write exams on a computer or be given extra time; an appeals process for failing scores is provided for when students have compelling circumstances), the timed writing system is the most time- and cost-efficient for assessing large numbers of students in a short period of time.

There are a number of objections to timed writing assessments for all students and for L2 writers in particular. Many writing experts feel that timed, high-pressure writing does not give any student the opportunity to demonstrate true proficiency (Kroll, 1990b; Silva, 1997) and others are concerned about validity problems inherent in scoring (McNamara, 1996; Purves, 1992; Weigle, 2002), problems that no amount of tinkering with rubrics and socialization processes seems to solve (Hamp-Lyons, 2003). As to L2 writers, the objection is raised that the time pressures place even more unfair burdens on them, as it is difficult to think and compose fluently and accurately in a second language, especially in a time-limited, high-stakes context (Kroll, 1990b). Some institutions have attempted to address this concern by allowing L2 writers additional time (as at my own university)—but in contexts where identification of L2 writers can be problematic, it can and does easily transpire that some L2 writers benefit from these extra considerations while others taking the same examination on the same day were unaware of this option. Some L2 specialists would further argue that even an extra allotment of time is not adequate to compensate for the severe strain that timed-writing assessments place on the abilities of L2 writers.[6]

In addition, most timed assessments require students to approach a writing topic/prompt "cold"—that is, with no advance preparation (Weigle, 2002). Under such circumstances, the nature of the task or writing prompt—its rhetorical structure, content, and language—can be extremely important and especially problematic for L2 writers, who may lack the cultural knowledge assumed by some prompts (CCCC, 2001) or be confused by specific task- or content-specific words or phrases in the prompt itself or in any source material provided (e.g., a short text that students must read and comment on): "When students are asked to write about unfamiliar content, they may be at a disadvantage" (Hamp-Lyons, 2003, pp. 170–171; see also discussion in Weigle, 2002). Thus, from an institutional perspective, it can be critical for assessment committees to include prompt writers with sensitivity to the needs of multilingual students.

What Skills Are Assessed?

A related question is what constitutes "proficiency" (for graduation) or "adequate progress/skills/ability" (for passing on to the next course level). In most cases, a scoring scale, which may be holistic, analytic, or trait-based, is used to assess the piece of writing being considered. There are many examples of such rubrics available in both L1 and L2 settings, and they typically consider multiple aspects of the text, including various issues related to content, organization, and language use (Ferris & Hedgcock, 2005; Hamp-Lyons, 2003; Weigle, 2002). When L2 writers are being assessed (whether in a separate L2 setting or together with L1 students), the question arises as to how much weight or attention will be given to students' strengths and weaknesses in language use (CCCC, 2001), and especially whether errors or language features most prototypically ESL will be penalized at one extreme or ignored at the other.

Alternative Assessment Options

Because of the problems with large-scale timed-writing assessment—both perceived and demonstrated—some institutions have developed alternative assessment models, such as portfolio assessment or successful completion of a writing course, to demonstrate writing proficiency for graduation. However, portfolio scoring can be cumbersome on the large scale, and adding writing courses is expensive, so most schools still use timed-writing assessments as their default option. In contrast, on the smaller scale (e.g., final assessments at the end of a course to see if students can move on to the next level), more programs are transitioning to less problematic approaches, which may include group reading of portfolios and/or consideration of students' overall performance in their classes (i.e., effort, reading assessments, and various types of written texts) rather than relying on a one-shot timed essay as the only indicator of what the student has learned in the writing or language course (Ferris & Hedgcock, 2005; Ferris, 2008; Hamp-Lyons, 2003).

Alternative assessment approaches or options can be extremely beneficial to all students, but are especially so for L2 writers, who arguably are the most disadvantaged by being forced to pass a timed writing assessment to stay in the university (in the case of state-mandated remediation deadlines), to pass their courses, or to graduate. Whether the decision is to allow students to prepare a portfolio at the end of a course rather than take a final essay examination or to give them the option of taking a writing course rather than a test to demonstrate proficiency for graduation, assessment mechanisms that emphasize process and development rather than one text produced at one point in time under extremely stressful conditions not only reduce student anxiety but give them their best chance to succeed—and not simply in jumping through the institutional hoop but in developing L2 language and writing proficiency (CCCC, 2001; Ferris, 2008; Silva, 1997).[7]

Who Should Score L2 Student Writing?

When students are enrolled in specialized ESL courses or sequences and must complete program- or course-wide final essay examinations or portfolio assessments, the answer to the *who* question is usually self-apparent: The instructors of those courses and perhaps their supervisor do the scoring, typically with papers distributed so that instructors do not grade their own students' work. Although there is still individual variation as to how grading standards are applied, a homogeneous group of L2-trained and/or experienced writing instructors generally ensures that L2 acquisition processes are taken into account and L2 features in writing are placed in perspective.

Dynamics change, however, when students are in less sheltered circumstances: L2 writers enrolled in mainstream courses (whether by their own choice or because they did not have an alternative option); course-wide exit assessments in which L1 and L2 papers or portfolios are graded together; and institutional examinations for placement and/or for graduation. In these various scenarios, L2 writers may be assessed by mainstream composition instructors, by L2 instructors who are part of the group-grading process, or even by faculty across the disciplines who have been hired as extra readers for a large institutional exam. Given the range of preparation, experience, and philosophies likely represented in such a mixed group of readers, there can be both benefits and problems for L2 writers being judged in these settings. Philosophically speaking, there are some potential benefits for all student writers when they are assessed by readers who represent a larger real-world audience than their own classroom writing instructors can provide for them; they gain an authentic sense of how their writing measures up against that of their peers and against the bias or sympathies of a diverse audience.

That said, many L1 composition specialists and even more disciplinary specialists have limited experience with and training in evaluating the texts of multilingual writers (Blanton, 1999; Frodesen & Starna, 1999). They may not realize (1) that second language acquisition is a lengthy, even lifelong, process; (2) that in the vast majority of cases, it is unrealistic and unfair to expect a text written by an L2 student to look exactly like those by monolingual native speakers; (3) that there are differences between and features peculiar to texts written by highly functional bilinguals and those written by incipient bilinguals (Frodesen & Starna, 1999; Valdés, 1992/2006); and (4) that ESL language features must be put into their proper perspective when weighed against other strengths and weaknesses in student texts. As already noted, the reactions to L2 writing by nonspecialists can range from overly harsh to excessively benign (e.g., giving students credit for their ideas even if the writing/language is quite flawed), and neither extreme is especially helpful for the overall development of L2 students.

As to assessment in particular, there are several approaches to the disconnect between L2 writers and these L1 teachers. One approach is to simply let students experience the real-world consequences of being assessed by native speakers who may or may not be sensitive to or sympathetic toward the challenges they face. The philosophy behind this approach is something like, "If they're going to get a degree from an English-speaking college/university and/or work professionally in an English-speaking environment, we cannot lower the standards for them: It's ethically wrong and it only cheats them in the long run." A nearly opposite approach is to have multilingual papers or portfolios graded separately by trained L2 writing specialists. The argument behind this approach is that it is not only unrealistic and unfair to judge L2 writing by standards designed for native speakers, but it is unethical to take students' money for several years and then put up an insurmountable roadblock (in the form of the assessment itself and unsympathetic, uninformed readers) to their further progress or graduation. A possible middle ground that attempts to address both sets of concerns is to grade L1 and L2 papers together but to carefully socialize all readers as to "passing" and "failing" L2 features that may be observed, with at least one "passing" paper written by a multilingual writer with obvious L2 features included in the training/norming packet. However, it is important to caution that this last approach is easier said than done, both because the experience and knowledge needed to accurately assess L2 writing cannot be gained in just a few minutes of training, and because even the training may not overcome the previously mentioned biases (or sympathies) that some readers may strongly hold (Hamp-Lyons, 2003; Weigle, 2002).

Assessment: Summary

Assessment is a critical issue to consider in designing and overseeing a writing or language program. Whether the purposes of program-wide assessment are for placement, end-of-term evaluation, or graduation, the way(s) in which these issues and questions are addressed will have a profound impact not only on the students themselves but on the types of courses and support services offered. Again, the point here is not to unduly criticize existing models but rather to observe that whatever approaches to assessment are taken will necessarily and inevitably impact a range of programmatic decisions.

Teacher Preparation

Once program administrators have wrestled with the issues of placement and assessment of L2 writers, a final question remains: Who teaches (or will teach or should teach) these student writers and what kinds of preparation do these instructors need to adequately serve a diverse and complex student audience? At post-secondary levels, this question pertains to at least three distinct groups of instructors:

1. teachers of courses designed especially for multilingual writers
2. teachers of composition courses designed primarily for monolingual L1 writers but which might also include some L2 students
3. teachers of writing courses across the disciplines

Further subcategories under Groups 1 and 2 might further include tutors working in writing or learning centers; under all groups might also be found adjunct tutors and instructors who provide additional support to students taking either composition courses or courses in the disciplines. Finally, of course, there are the instructors of courses across the curriculum that do not *focus* on writing but that *include* writing as a major part of the assessment scheme.

Teachers of Multilingual/L2 Writing Classes

Where programs do offer separate courses for multilingual writers, one of the most important benefits claimed is that students are taught by instructors who are sensitized to their needs and trained to meet them. As noted by Matsuda in a number of recent publications (e.g., 1999, 2006b), L2 writing is a field that draws from two disciplines, composition studies and second language (or applied linguistics or TESOL) studies. While many L2 writing teachers tend to have TESOL training (which may or may not have included specific preparation on teaching L2 writing), others have come from composition training programs and have developed an interest and/or on-the-job expertise in working with multilingual writers.

This merging of disciplines and of the two groups of L2 writing teachers has both advantages and challenges. TESOL-trained instructors may have strong preparation in linguistics and in SLA theory, thus providing them with an understanding of language issues that arise in student writing and of acquisition processes that may help or hinder their students' writing development. However, they may not have had much (or any) training in composition theory and pedagogy and may, as a result, approach the task primarily as language teachers rather than writing teachers (Zamel, 1985), focusing heavily on grammar and vocabulary rather than on composing processes and audience analysis. In contrast, instructors with composition training may be well equipped to teach writing but underprepared to work with diverse students. As a result, they may misunderstand and underestimate the struggles and barriers L2 writers face, often ignoring or neglecting their need for continued language development. Even if they do understand students' language needs, their own professional preparation program may not have adequately trained them to address these issues.[8]

Clearly, both ends of the language/writing continuum are important, so the ideal L2 writing teacher would have substantial training in both second language development and in writing pedagogy (CCCC, 2001; Matsuda, 1999; Wurr, 2004). As noted by Wurr (2004):

> . . . a more comprehensive, integrated, and unified approach to composition instruction and professional training is necessary. Integrating L1 and L2 composition theory and practice more consistently in English studies would better prepare professionals in the field for today's linguistically diverse classrooms and communities. *Graduate programs in rhetoric and composition need to include and require more courses in TESOL and second language writing,* while *programs in applied linguistics need to increase the number of graduates specializing in TESOL and second language writing* in order to better meet the need for specialists in these fields in American higher education. (p. 19, emphasis added)

In short, while many L2 writing professionals have developed substantial expertise and skill over the years, the sub-field of second language writing still has some distance to travel in articulating appropriate goals and mechanisms for preparing teachers of L2 writers and especially in implementing such goals programmatically.

Teachers of Mainstream Composition Courses

If it is still relatively uncommon for L2 professionals to have specialized training in teaching writing, it is even rarer for composition instructors to have specific preparation in working with multilingual writers. If classes in teaching second language writers are available, they are usually offered through the TESOL program, not the composition program, and pre-service composition teachers at most have the option of taking a TESOL-sponsored writing course as an elective in their teacher-preparation program. Rare indeed are graduate programs in rhetoric/composition that require coursework that prepares future writing teachers to learn more about second language issues. In 2001, the Conference on College Composition and Communication (CCCC) approved a position statement entitled "Statement on Second Language Writing and Second Language Writers," which includes the following:

> *We also urge graduate programs in writing-related fields to offer courses in second-language writing theory, research, and instruction* in order to prepare writing teachers and scholars for working with a college student population that is increasingly diverse both linguistically and culturally. (CCCC, 2001, emphasis added)

Later in the position statement, an even stronger recommendation is made:

> Any writing course—including basic writing, first-year composition, advanced writing, and professional writing as well as second-language writing courses—*that enrolls any second-language writers* should be taught by a writing teacher who is able to identify and is prepared to address the linguistic and cultural needs of second-language writers. (CCCC, 2001, emphasis added)

Though many programs around the United States and elsewhere have made progress in recent years in offering pre-service and in-service training on second language writing issues to composition instructors, the "disciplinary division of labor" (between composition and ESL/TESOL programs) articulated and chronicled by Matsuda (1999, 2006b) is still firmly established in most contexts. One fairly typical anecdote from my own experience should illustrate this. For some years I participated in my department's interviews for new composition lecturers, including those who would teach mainstream courses, multilingual courses, or both. Several years ago I asked to have added to the interview protocol a question on how the candidate would address the needs of multilingual writers in his/her classroom. In a recent round of interviews, one otherwise strong interviewee responded to this question by saying, "I'm not trained in ESL, so I would send those students to the Writing Center or to obtain private tutoring." Though other candidates provided more adequate responses (e.g., they would give those students more individual help; they would find out about their native languages), that candidate was nonetheless hired over my objections.

Concerns and recommendations about the preparation of those who teach mainstream composition courses that include multilingual writers also extend to tutors in campus writing/learning centers, adjunct tutorials linked to writing courses or courses in the disciplines, and other types of support services. Such programs are typically staffed by upper-division and graduate students, and these students may find themselves working with multilingual writers (who in some contexts are the majority clientele of the center or program) with little or no preparation for doing so. As noted by Leki (2004):

> Stories abound of tutor disinclination to work with ESL writers because these students do not fit the profile of the students the tutor was trained to help; their differing needs and expectations have made tutors feel incompetent and sometimes even annoyed. L2 writers have their share of complaints as well: tutors who seem to know nothing about the structures of English that the writer seeks help with; tutors who seem to insist on dealing with nebulously broad issues of organization or development; tutors who seem to refuse to give the kind of help that writers feel they need. *What should be an ideal encounter for helping L2 writers move forward with their writing morphs into frustration* for both tutors and writers. (p. xi, emphasis added)

Ideally, one-on-one tutorial sessions or small group adjunct tutorials should be extremely helpful support mechanisms for L2 writers in higher education: They have the potential to provide the extended, individualized assistance that is responsive to students' unique writing needs and background knowledge (or lack thereof), that is far less feasible in larger classroom settings (even in multilingual writing courses). However, if programs and tutors are unwilling and/or unable to focus on the specialized needs of second language writers (see Bruce, 2004; Linville, 2004), these support systems may, as Leki describes, not only fail to achieve the potential benefits but yield mainly frustration for all concerned. Programs in some contexts have addressed these issues by ensuring that writing/learning centers include second language writing experts on their staff as well as diverse peer tutors who can serve as role models for academic success (see e.g., Destandau & Wald, 2002; Wolfe-Quintero & Segade, 1999). However, especially in academic settings that include many multilingual writers with a wide range of backgrounds, *all* tutors need some kind of preparation for working with L2 writers. Internship and practicum courses should include such training as an integral course component (extending far beyond the typical "ESL day" found in many such courses), writing/learning center materials and libraries should include high-quality materials for use with L2 writers, and center staff and tutors should be able to consult regularly with L2 writing experts.

Teachers of Courses in the Disciplines

The most difficult teacher preparation issues relate to instructors outside of English/ESL/writing programs. Beyond first-year composition and other writing requirements, multilingual students will take general education and discipline-specific courses that require writing of various types. Such courses are taught by disciplinary experts rather than composition or ESL professionals. Disciplinary faculty have the benefit of neither language nor composition training, so their pedagogy as to writing instruction and assessment, their knowledge of L2 issues, and their expectations of what student writing should look like may all be lacking, inadequate, and/or inaccurate. Harklau, Siegal, & Losey (1999) note that it is faculty in the disciplines who most need to be educated about the characteristics of L2 writers and their texts, further noting, "there must be institution-wide willingness to accept responsibility for English learners' development as college writers . . . it is indeed a difficult matter to change faculty attitudes and practices regarding writing in higher education settings" (pp. 11–12).

Wolfe-Quintero and Segade (1999) argue at length that multilingual students' language and writing development must be seen as a process that extends across students' higher education careers, noting that both ESL students and faculty in the disciplines at their institution (the University of Hawaii) felt that the freshman composition course had not prepared the students adequately for writing in their major courses. They further state that the solution is "a recognition that *writing ability is developed through an entire undergraduate education* through a variety of means of university support and that L2 students have unique language needs that *require assistance throughout their undergraduate career*" (p. 196, emphases added). This recommendation is echoed in the position statement published by CCCC (2001).

Many institutions in recent years have recognized the needs for "writing in the disciplines/writing across the curriculum" (WID/WAC) programs, have revamped undergraduate curricula to require and provide more writing instruction, and have hired WID/WAC specialists (usually with Composition/Rhetoric training) to provide workshops and assistance to disciplinary faculty as they assign and assess student writing. Less apparent, however, is the incorporation of training for faculty across the disciplines to work with L2 writers (Browning et al., 2000).

Teacher preparation with regard to L2 writers is a complex issue. There is a substantial knowledge, skill, and experience base to be mastered both for *writing* instruction and for *second language* instruction. Despite the evolution of second language writing as a field that draws from both composition and second language studies, most teachers of L2 writers—whether they be TESOL-trained, composition-trained, or experts in their own disciplines—have not had adequate preparation for the challenging endeavor of working effectively with second language writers. Since the teacher is a critical variable in *any* instructional setting, this is no small matter. The important issue of teacher preparation will be discussed again in Chapter 6.

Chapter 3 has examined the interacting issues of *curriculum, placement, assessment,* and *teacher preparation* with regard to the different audiences of L2 students at colleges and universities today. We have observed that the blurring boundaries between "native and non-native speaker" raise a number of questions regarding the identification and appropriate placement of L2 students into various types of courses and that the distinctions among multilingual students lead to further implications as to whether or not all multilingual students belong together in specialized courses. We have further seen that assessment and teacher preparation issues need to be carefully explored and resolved, not only in writing programs themselves but across the disciplines and for institutional assessments such as writing proficiency requirements for graduation. As traditional categories and dividing lines among student audiences become increasingly inaccurate and even unhelpful in some cases, administrators and instructors in post-secondary settings must work together to develop new terminology, new procedures, and new models.

QUESTIONS FOR REFLECTION AND DISCUSSION

1. This chapter might initially appear to be relevant only to writing program administrators and curriculum or assessment experts. Is it important for classroom instructors to understand big-picture issues of curriculum, placement, assessment, and teacher preparation? Why or why not?

2. The issue of whether separate ESL writing/language course options ought to be available at the college level (i.e., beyond the "remedial" course) is controversial. What are your opinions about this? Should college-level L2 writers always be mainstreamed with L1 peers, or should separate sections be available to them?

3. This chapter takes a strong position with regard to *student choice*, arguing especially that L2 students ought to have the final decision about whether to enroll in mainstream or L2 courses if both options are available. Do you agree with this position, and if not, how would you modify it?

4. For large-scale writing assessment, who do you think should grade L2 students' texts—L2 specialists only, or a combination of readers? Why do you hold this view?

5. The section on teacher preparation takes the position that most "mainstream" instructors (in composition and in specific disciplines) need more training to better serve L2 students. Do you agree with this stance? Do you have any concerns about it?

CHAPTER ENDNOTES

[1] Once again, I acknowledge and agree with comments of authors such as Chiang and Schmida (1999); Frodesen & Starna (1999); Goen et al. (2002); Harklau, Siegal, & Losey (1999); Valdés (1992/2006); and Wurr (2004) regarding the blurring of boundaries between "native" and "nonnative" students that is occurring. However, for this particular discussion, since many programs *do* characterize their offerings in terms of divisions such as "ESL vs. native English speaker" or "ESL vs. basic writing vs. mainstream/college-level composition courses," the labels are transparent and provide a framework for discussion.

[2] At some institutions, students are given credit for ESL courses (even those below the college level as to composition) as fulfilling "foreign language" requirements, the argument being that even "remedial" ESL classes at colleges/universities require more L2 proficiency than do lower-division "college-level" foreign language courses—so ESL students should get credit for continued L2 English development in the same way that monolingual English students get credit for taking, say, beginning French courses. See Silva (1997) and Lay et al. (1999) for more discussion of the noncredit issue.

[3] Costino and Hyon (2007) also mention that at their CSU campus, multilingual students who are U.S.-born are not sent letters offering a choice between multilingual and mainstream sections of basic writing courses.

[4] It is also the case in this program that once multilingual students have taken the in-house placement examination, they can be directed to an extra (lower-level) course that is not required of students in the mainstream program. While this additional course requirement may well be in the long-term best interests of the students, the unintended and unfortunate consequence of this unequal treatment is that some multilingual students opt for the mainstream composition track, regardless of whether a multilingual course placement might be better for them.

[5] There might be disagreement, however, as to at what level multilingual options should end. For example, in the program described by Costino and Hyon (2007), there are two levels of separate basic writing courses prior to first-year composition, and there are multilingual sections of those basic writing classes. However, once students reach the first-year composition level, they are mainstreamed. In other programs, there are equivalent first-year composition multilingual sections available, and even multilingual writing courses at the upper-division and graduate levels as well.

[6] Students who have "official" L2 standing at my previous institution get four hours to complete the WPE, in contrast with the 2 ½ hours mainstream writers receive. Even so, their overall pass rate on the exam is lower than that of the native speakers, and their texts in general are much more problematic.

[7] As I have written elsewhere, in our program we transitioned one of our courses several years ago from a final essay examination to a portfolio assessment, and the results were dramatic: Our pass rate nearly doubled, and more importantly, the quality of student effort, engagement, and written products improved instantly (Ferris, 2008).

[8] I recently was asked to give a guest lecture to a class that prepared interns to do peer tutoring in the campus writing center. I talked specifically about the sentence- and word-level needs of multilingual writers and ways in which one-to-one tutoring was ideally suited to give students the kind of focused attention to these issues that many classroom teachers rarely have time to provide. The interns listened politely, and then one raised her hand: "All your suggestions involve working with grammar issues, but I don't know anything about grammar. How can I possibly help multilingual writers with their language problems?" I was taken aback by this glaringly obvious question and bit back my first response: "If you are going to be a writing instructor, you *must* learn about grammar!"

Appendix   Sample Student Questionnaire for Identification & Placement of Multilingual Writers

1. Is English your second (or third or fourth) language?_____
   - What is your first language (= the language you spoke at home with your parents as a young child)? _____
   - List your previous schooling
     ◦ In your first language: grade ____ through grade ____
     ◦ Total years: _____
     ◦ In English: grade _____ through grade _____
     ◦ Total years (or months): _____
   - Where were you born?
     ◦ U.S. _____
     ◦ Parents' home country (which one?):_____

2. Did you graduate from a U.S. high school? Yes_____ No_____

3. If the answer to #2 is "No," are you an international student? Yes_____ No_____
   - TOEFL score: _____
   - TWE score:_____
   - English language study: Yes_____ No_____
     ◦ If yes, where?_____
     ◦ How long?_____

4. If the answer to #2 is "Yes":
   - Which high school?_____
   - What year?_____
   - Did you take ESL classes before college? Yes_____ No_____
     If "yes," when and where:
     _____elementary school (# of years:_____)
     _____middle/junior high school (# of years:_____)
     _____high school (# of years:_____)

5. How do you use your languages? Please complete the chart below. Do not include languages you only studied in school as a required subject but only languages you use regularly. For each category, fill in 1 = well; 2 = some; or 3 = not much:

Language	Understand	Speak	Read	Write
1. English				
2.				

6. Overall, my best language is: _____

7. For my college writing classes, I would be more comfortable in:
   _____classes which include both native and nonnative speakers of English
   _____classes for multilingual/ESL students

8. How do you feel about reading/writing in English? Check the answer that best expresses your feelings or opinion:
   _____confident _____OK _____anxious _____terrible

9. What do you think are your greatest needs or weaknesses in reading/writing in English? (If you can't think of anything, leave it blank.)

Adapted from Goen et al., 2002, and Reid, 1998/2006b.

Chapter 4

Different L2 Audiences and Course Design Options

<table>
<tr><td>

Students have two areas in which they must improve—language and academic reading and writing skills—and . . . the university needs to give them time, focused instruction, and expert faculty to work on these things simultaneously.
—Holten, 2002, p. 176

</td><td>

CHAPTER 3 DISCUSSED PROGRAM-WIDE IMPLICA-tions that arise from our understanding of the three student audiences discussed in Part 1. Chapter 4 moves to a more specific topic, the design of individual courses to address the academic language needs of L2 students discussed in some detail in Chapter 2 (see especially Figs. 2.4.–2.5). Rather than generally discussing course design for L2 literacy (for examples, see Aebersold & Field, 1997; Ferris & Hedgcock, 2005; Hedgcock & Ferris, 2009), this chapter

</td></tr>
</table>

focuses specifically on the issues raised in Part 1 of this book. First, courses designed especially and exclusively for multilingual students are discussed, followed by special considerations for courses composed of both mainstream (monolingual English speakers) and multilingual readers/writers.

Topics and Initial Assumptions

Chapter 4 focuses on six specific areas (see Fig. 4.1) of course design: (1) needs analysis; (2) goal-setting; (3) tasks and topics; (4) materials selection; (5) specific language instruction; and (6) classroom assessment and grading practices. For all sub-topics, assume that courses are being designed for two- or four-year college settings in the United States or other English-medium contexts; that they are fundamentally "academic" in nature (i.e., not focused on conversational, survival, or workplace English skills); that they primarily emphasize academic literacy development; and, finally, that individual instructors have adequate time, freedom, and preparation to undertake a thorough and thoughtful course-planning process.[1]

FIGURE 4.1
Summary of Course Design Issues and Questions for the Three Audiences

Phase of Course Design Process	Questions to Consider
Needs analysis	What do I know about the backgrounds of the students in this class, and what might be their most pressing needs? How do their characteristics and needs intersect with institutional or departmental objectives for and constraints upon this course?
Goal-setting	Given the make-up of *this particular group of students,* what are the most important academic literacy objectives to address?
Tasks and topics	What are the most important types of reading/writing tasks for these students, and what topics might be most appropriate for them?
Materials selection	What are the most appropriate materials for intensive and/or extensive reading for this group of students, given the course goals?
Specific language instruction	On what language skills does this group need to focus, and how will language issues factor into the overall course plan?
Assessment and grading	Given the needs of this group of students and the course goals, on what types of tasks and skills will assessment instruments and the grading scheme focus? Will the assessment scheme need to be adjusted to reflect the varying abilities of different sub-groups of students in the class?

Needs Analysis

It should be readily apparent from the extended discussions in previous chapters that needs analysis, while always critical in any teaching context, is especially so in settings in which the characteristics of the target student audience(s) are diverse and complex. Even experienced teachers of L2 students must re-orient themselves to the needs of a shifting student population. In my own case, over the course of a 25-year career working with L2 writers in various institutions, I have moved from teaching primarily international students to late-arriving residents to an increasing number of early-arriving students. The training and experience of my early years had inculcated a number of (often false) assumptions in my mind about ESL students:

- All ESL students know a lot about grammar.

- Students will misunderstand and resist nearly all elements of the writing process, including (or especially) multiple-drafting and revision, peer response, fluency activities such as freewriting and journaling, and a decreased focus on language/grammar issues.

- Students will enjoy writing about topics about their home country or culture and/or comparing the home country to the L2 country.

- Students will be able to read, comprehend, and analyze fairly challenging short texts.

- Students will have trouble with spoken English, so I need to speak slowly and clearly and avoid slang and idiom usage and provide a lot of visual support. They also will be shy and fearful about speaking in class or speaking individually with the teacher.

- Students want all of their written errors corrected by me, and they will be able to understand correction symbols and verbal rule reminders that I write on their texts.

Of course, even in working with mostly/all international students, I found considerable variation with regard to the truth of the belief system I had adopted. For example, students from some cultures with strong oral traditions were quite willing and able to talk in class and interact freely with me and with each other, but they had limited L2 literacy experience and severe difficulties with matters such as spelling, simple sentence construction, and basic mechanics (e.g., capitalization, margins, and terminal punctuation). In short, despite being "elective bilinguals" (Valdés, 1992/2006) and international students, their language skills were more like those of the "ear" learners described by Reid (1997, 2006a, 1998/2006b). Even the more traditional "eye" learners among my students varied from one another as to grammar knowledge, reading ability, and listening/speaking skills, depending on individuals' learning styles, personality types, motivation sources, and prior educational experiences.

Nonetheless, my list of assumptions/stereotypes/myths functioned fairly well for me until I changed institutions and began teaching an audience of mostly late-arriving residents, as defined in Chapter 1. The need for change became clear to me quickly through two experiences in ESL writing classrooms my first year in the new context. One day, I had my students in groups of three, providing peer editing assistance to one another. As I eavesdropped on the groups, I heard a disagreement about a writer's use of the verb phrase *had made*. One assertive young woman insisted that the correct form should be **had maded* (an * means it's ungrammatical), adding that she had been in the United States since she was seven so she should know. The other students, far more recent arrivals, quickly submitted to her "superior" knowledge, and the writer actually was about to "correct" his text as she had directed, until I intervened. In the second example, I was leading a class discussion about subject-verb agreement and tried to elicit from my students what the term meant. One late-arriving resident student raised his hand and helpfully offered, "If the noun has an *s* on the end, the verb needs to have one, too—so they agree!" In both instances, I realized that my prior assumptions about students' explicit and formal grammatical knowledge were incorrect for this audience and that I had to take a different approach, one that stepped back and defined terms such as *noun, verb, subject, singular,* and *plural* before I could talk about how subjects and verbs "agree."

Another eye-opening moment for me that first year was when my students forcefully expressed how tired they were of assignments that asked them to compare some aspect of their home culture/country to that of the United States. Some of them had been in the United States for a number of years and had left their home country in early adolescence; their memories and comparisons seemed out-of-date, uninteresting, and irrelevant to their current situation. In short, I quickly learned that the background knowledge and strategies I had relied on in my years of teaching international students had to shift dramatically.

During the time that I taught at the same institution for nearly 20 years, the L2 student audience changed substantially. Over my final ten years there, a growing proportion of the students in the ESL (now called "multilingual") program were early-arrivals who were also found in all of the mainstream writing classes in the department. These students, as suggested in Chapter 1, were fully assimilated to American classrooms, spoke English fluently and in some cases without an accent, and had strong listening comprehension skills. However, they were not generally strong readers, knew little-to-nothing about formal English grammar, and tended to write more informally and conversationally than was expected at the college level. They did not need me to slow or simplify my speaking style or avoid idioms or references to popular culture, but they did need me to help them develop appropriate and effective academic literacy skills. At the same time, because all three audiences (i.e., international, late-arriving, and early-arriving students) were still present in the program (albeit in differing proportions than in the past), I could not forget what I had previously learned about the knowledge, skills, and needs of international students or late-arriving residents.

Since all teachers will encounter different groups of students in various "mixes" in their own contexts, it is important to ask the right questions about a specific institution, course, and target audience prior to planning and teaching a course.

This is also helpful information for program administrators to convey to teachers, especially new instructors, and perhaps to include in a faculty handbook. Sample questions to consider are listed in Figure 4.2.

FIGURE 4.2

Sample Needs Analysis Questions about Programs and Courses

About the Institution

- Approximately how many international students are there, and from what regions/ countries? Are they mostly graduate or undergraduate students? What TOEFL scores are required for admission?
- Among resident L2 students, what proportion are late arrivals or early arrivals? What are typical ages of arrival in the U.S., and how long has the average immigrant student been in this country? What are their countries/regions of origin (or their parents')?
- How are multilingual students identified, assessed, and placed into writing/English/ ESL courses?
- Are there institution-wide writing assessments for initial placement and/or for graduation? What other writing requirements are there? Who assesses/teaches multilingual students, what kinds of tasks are those students given, and what are the scoring/grading criteria?
- Outside of regular writing/English/ESL classes, what other support services are available for multilingual students?

About the Specific Course

- What are the prerequisites, entrance, and exit requirements for this course? What courses do students take before this one, and where do they go after this course?
- Are there general course-wide or departmental curricular objectives and/or grading criteria? Are these available for instructors to examine?
- Are there specific requirements for this course that should affect course planning, such as number/type of assignments, number of words produced, etc.? Are there any published materials that specify these?
- Are there course-wide or program-wide assessments during or at the end of this course? What is the nature of the assessment(s), who grades them, and how much impact do they have on students' course outcomes? Would it be possible for teachers to observe a scoring session and/or examine sample essay prompts, previous student exams, etc.?
- Are there any texts/materials that are required or have been effective for this particular course? Any tasks or assignments that work well?
- Are there experienced teachers of this course that new teachers could observe or talk to? Are there any current or recent students new teachers could talk to? Are there any samples of student texts written for this course that new teachers could look at?

FIGURE 4.2 (continued)

About the Students in the Course

- What is the usual profile of students in this course? What is their status (e.g., visa, permanent resident, U.S.-born)? What L1s are usually represented? What is their typical age range?
- What are their educational backgrounds? Did they attend English classes in a home country, did they attend U.S. K–12 schools, adult school, community college, or intensive/private language programs?
- Are most students in this course full-time students? How many units do they usually take? Do they have jobs outside of school, family responsibilities, etc. that will limit the time they can spend on this course?
- What are students' abilities, strengths, or proficiency levels in English language/literacy? Are there any sample texts, reading assessment scores, etc., from current or recent students that I could examine?
- What kinds of previous instruction have students had in English grammar, in academic essay structure, in the writing process, or in reading strategies? Is there anything I can assume they know (or don't know)?
- What are students' views, attitudes, and feeling about reading and writing academic English? What types of classroom activities do they respond well to, and what do they resist?
- Do most students have easy access to computers and the Internet? Are they typically fairly proficient in using technology for literacy instruction?

Though some of the questions in Figure 4.2 would be part of any good needs analysis, others are designed especially with the understanding that different student audiences (or several audiences co-occurring in the same context) will necessitate asking specific questions and designing courses and classroom instruction (see Chapter 5) in unique ways.

Goal-Setting

Most experienced teachers and course designers are well aware that the careful articulation of course goals is a critical preliminary step in the course-planning process (Aebersold & Field, 1997; Ferris & Hedgcock, 2005; Hedgcock & Ferris, 2009; Murphy & Byrd, 2001). As one old saying goes, "Aim at nothing, and you are sure to hit it." Some years ago I was being interviewed for a teaching job at a university intensive ESL program, and I asked a question about the course goals or curriculum for the class I was being hired to teach. The interviewer responded in all seriousness, "The goal of Level 1 is to finish the textbook so that students will be ready for Level 2." While "finish the textbook" is a straightforward and probably achievable goal, we would hope that most program designers and instructors would think more deeply about the goal-setting process. Identifying course objectives involves consideration of several issues, including evaluation of dominant instructional approaches (Figure 4.3) and the characteristics and needs of all L2 students/writers (see the following discussion and Chapter 2).

FIGURE 4.3
Overview of Major Approaches in L2 Reading and Writing

Approach	Focus	Representative Techniques
Intensive reading	In-class work on a short text to facilitate comprehension and develop and practice reading and writing strategies	Previewing/predicting, skimming, scanning, summarizing, vocabulary and other language work
Extensive reading	Reading quantities of self-selected text for enjoyment and general understanding	Sustained silent reading, reading logs, book groups, poster presentations
Controlled or guided composition	Manipulation of language to produce well-formed sentences and paragraphs	Changing a text from past to present tense or from first to third person; constructing a paragraph based on a list of details and/or following a model
Paragraph-pattern composition	Producing well-structured paragraphs and essays in specific rhetorical modes (e.g., narration, description, compare/contrast, etc.)	Writing topic or thesis statements; learning the structure of an introduction, body, and conclusion; connections between paragraphs; outlining; analyzing sample texts
Process approach to composition	Helping the writer to discover and develop effective processes; student "ownership," "engagement," and "voice"	Prewriting, freewriting, drafting, revision, feedback; collaboration, portfolio assessment
English for Academic Purposes composition	Understanding and meeting the needs of a given audience or "academic discourse community"	Assignment analysis across the curriculum; incorporating sources; using appropriate academic vocabulary and grammatical structures

Sources: Ferris & Hedgcock, 2005; Johns, 1990; Matsuda, 2006b; Raimes, 1991; Silva, 1990.

Historical Approaches to Teaching L2 Writing

Over the past half-century, approaches to the teaching of L2 writers have moved through at least four distinct phases (Ferris & Hedgcock, 2005; Matsuda, 2003b, 2006b; Raimes, 1991; Silva, 1990), although it is fair to say that elements of all four still (co-)exist in many programs, courses, and textbooks today. In its earliest stages, "writing" was seen primarily as a means to practice grammar and vocabulary learned in language classes, often through "controlled" or "guided" composition exercises in which the content and structure of the text was provided to students and they were asked to manipulate specific language features, such as changing narratives from present to past tense or from first person to third. Later, in response to Kaplan's (1966) pioneering article on *contrastive rhetoric,* which followed the rise of *current-traditional* rhetoric in composition teaching, L2 student writers were presented with (and asked to emulate) typical English paragraph and essay patterns. This has been called the "paragraph-pattern approach" (see Raimes, 1985; Matsuda, 2003b; Silva & Matsuda, 2002). In the 1970s, led again by L1 composition trends and by an early article on ESL writing by Zamel (1976), teachers began to turn their attention toward the *processes* involved as individuals produced texts, including invention strategies, multiple drafting, and revision. Finally, scholars in the 1980s, beginning with Horowitz (1986), began to question whether previous approaches to writing instruction adequately prepared L2 writers to produce discourse in various specialized academic disciplines, leading to approaches focusing on discourse genres under the rubric of English for Academic (or Specific) Purposes (EAP) (Swales, 1990; Johns, 1997, 1999). As memorably noted by Silva (1990), this "merry-go-round of approaches" generated "more heat than light" (p. 18); all four emphases variously represent aspects of writing that are real and significant, if perhaps out of balance within a specific approach considered in isolation.

As these historical approaches relate to the discussion of the three student audiences, their various aspects become particularly relevant in some instances and less so in others. For example, early-arriving resident L2 students, who have been acquiring English naturalistically most or all of their lives, most likely have little need at the college level for any elements of the controlled/guided composition approach; their intuitions about basic vocabulary and sentence patterns in English are well established, and they would not benefit much from such a low-level, tightly structured approach to writing instruction. In some cases, they may also have experienced elements of the process approach, such as revision and peer response, in secondary and even elementary U.S. classrooms, so they may not need as much explanation and justification for these activities as would new arrivals from other countries. However, as early-arriving students, for reasons discussed in Chapter 1, often arrive in college with inadequate academic literacy skills, the techniques and principles of English for Specific (Academic) Purposes (ESP) approach may be very appropriate and necessary for their success in post-secondary studies (Holten, 2002; Muchisky & Tangren, 1999; Reid, 2008; Roberge, 2002).

In contrast to the early-arriving resident audience, L2 students more newly arrived and/or with limited prior exposure to the English language and/or English writing may benefit, at least in the early stages of their studies, from some of the activities subsumed under the controlled composition or paragraph-pattern approaches. In the graduate master's TESOL courses I teach, I have sometimes found that the international graduate students are among the strongest academic writers: Their texts are well structured, logical, and clear. When asked how, as L2 writers, they developed these skills, which in many instances are stronger than those of their native English–speaking counterparts, most will tell stories of ESL writing instruction at an intensive English program or community college that taught them the basics of how to put an English paragraph or essay together (i.e., using paragraph-pattern techniques and principles). Although these graduate students have moved beyond the basic academic paragraph or essay and are capable of much more sophisticated analysis, they believe that the highly structured approach of these early ESL composition classes helped them to take their limited knowledge or/exposure to the English language and use it to produce acceptable basic English texts, successes on which they could then build with more demanding tasks and content. In short, understanding the characteristics of various L2 student groups can help instructors to choose and prioritize elements of the various approaches to L2 writing instruction that would be most relevant and useful to their particular student audience(s).

General Characteristics of L2 Student Writers

As also mentioned in Chapter 2, several reviewers and researchers over the years have attempted descriptions of L2 writers and their texts, in particular how L2 text is different than, or unique from, those written by monolingual native speakers. For example, Silva (1993) discussed findings in his review of 73 studies suggesting that for L2 writers, "L2 composing is more constrained, more difficult, and less effective" (p. 668). If this is true, there may be a range of reasons behind it: (1) a lack of lexical and syntactic resources, (2) a lack of knowledge of global organizational patterns at the text or paragraph level, (3) inadequate background knowledge about the subject matter because of differences in cultural and educational background, and (4) a lack of prior composition training either in the United States or in the home country (Ferris & Hedgcock, 2005; Hyland, 2002; Leki, 1992; see also Chapters 1–2). Summarizing many of these lines of research comparing L1 and L2 writers, Hyland notes that

- Advanced L2 writers are handicapped more by a lack of composing competence than linguistic competence. The opposite is true for lower-proficiency learners.
- L1 writing strategies may or may not be transferred to L2 contexts.
- L2 writers tend to plan less than L1 writers and produce shorter texts.

- L2 writers have more difficulty setting goals and generating material.
- L2 writers revise more but reflect less on their writing.
- L2 writers are less fluent and produce less accurate and effective texts.
- L2 writers are less inhibited by teacher editing and feedback. (2002, p. 36)

These generalizations are important especially in contexts, programs, or classes in which diverse L2 student audiences are taught together (Matsuda, 2008). While the implications of the differences in student characteristics are important—and indeed are the entire reason behind this book—it is also valuable and practical to acknowledge that there are certain issues and needs common to *all* L2 writers, such as the need to master effective composing strategies and the need to write more fluently and produce more linguistically accurate texts.

Course Goals for the Different L2 Audiences

With this background discussion in mind, we can begin to speculate about course goals that might differ across various student populations and those that would be similar for all L2 writers. Figure 4.4 provides a model for how such questions could be addressed in course planning. While this list is not intended to be exhaustive, it illustrates a range of different reading/writing course goals that might be variously represented in college-level courses that focus on L2 writers.

Balancing the Needs of Different Student Audiences

The obvious question that arises is how a teacher considers different student needs in the same classroom when designing a particular course. While specific classroom techniques will be discussed in more detail in Chapter 5, at this point we can observe that each class and context is different and that individual teachers will need to consider the various proportions and characteristics of their unique settings. For instance, if a class is heavily composed of international "eye" learners and has only a handful of resident students, the teacher might proceed by focusing on the needs and knowledge base of the majority (e.g., assuming a certain amount of grammatical knowledge or a lack of knowledge of English academic essay structure or of process approach strategies) and filling in gaps or adjusting expectations as needed for the other students. For instance, a teacher in this setting might provide extra grammar materials (handouts, websites, etc.) to the "ear" learners but not spend class time teaching grammar mini-lessons on concepts that most of the students already studied in English classes in their home countries. In contrast, a teacher with a majority population of early-arriving resident students might select a class reading that includes slang, idioms, and current cultural refer-

FIGURE 4.4
Sample Course Goals, Approaches, and Target Audience(s)

Sample Goal: *Students will be able to . . .*	Composition Approach(es) Illustrated	Most Appropriate or Significant Target Audience(s)
Write well-formed sentences and paragraphs	Controlled composition and paragraph-pattern	International & late-arriving resident
Produce well-structured academic essays	Paragraph-pattern	All
Read a variety of academic texts critically and with good comprehension	EAP	All, but especially early- and late-arriving "ear" learners
Develop, improve, and reflect upon their own writing processes and strategies	Process approach	All, but especially international students
Develop and effectively use knowledge of academic vocabulary and sophisticated sentence structure	EAP	All, but especially early- and late-arriving resident students
Paraphrase, summarize, analyze, and synthesize a variety of sources and integrate them effectively into their own texts	EAP	All, but especially "ear" (early- and late-arriving immigrant) learners
Write a variety of formal and informal texts with fluency, confidence, and enjoyment	Process approach	International students and "eye" learner late-arriving resident
Understand important grammar terms and rules and use them to self-edit their writing and apply teacher feedback in revision	Controlled composition & EAP	"Ear" learners (early-arriving and some/most late-arriving resident)

Figure 4.5
Task and Topic Questions and Options

Question	Options
What general reading/writing task types should be considered?	**Formal assignments:** Personal narrative; expository, persuasive, primary or secondary research, literary analysis **Informal writing:** journals/blogs, freewriting, written homework exercises
What general topical models should be considered?	Linked/thematic assignments (some or all writing tasks on the same topic) "General" academic writing Writing for specific disciplines
What kinds of topic/content are best for L2 audiences?	Content (texts and topics) culturally and linguistically accessible for L2 students Student-selected or student choice of topics "Newcomer" vs. "immigrant" experience topics "Universal" human-interest topics

ences, knowing that these students' long-term residence in the target culture will make this material familiar and accessible—but also provide a glossary or cultural knowledge handout for the few international or recently arrived resident students. The key in each situation is for the teacher to understand the *general* needs of all L2 readers/writers, the more *specific* characteristics of particular audiences and how those interact with course goals and classroom practices, and the *unique* circumstances presented in his/her own classroom and institutional context. Again, the needs analysis process and questions provided earlier in this chapter provide a framework for such decision-making. See Figure 4.5.

Tasks and Topics

Once a course designer or individual instructor has obtained information through needs analysis and has begun to articulate appropriate course goals, the next logical step is to identify and define specific task- and topic-types that will best move students toward the goals and enable the instructor to assess how well those goals have been met. In a reading/writing course, these task-types provide the general structure for the course and the framework for a more detailed week-to-week course syllabus. While a great deal has been written on reading/writing tasks in L2 literacy instruction (see, e.g., Aebersold & Field, 1997; Ferris & Hedgcock, 2005; Hedgcock & Ferris, 2009; Hirvela, 2004; Hudson, 2007; Johns, 1999; Kroll & Reid, 1994; Leki, 1993; Reid & Kroll, 1995; Reid, 2006a; Seymour & Walsh, 2006), here we move from these more general discussions to issues specifically related to the three student audiences.

Tasks

In college-level writing courses, there are several typical models of general task design. One is to expose students to a variety of genres and task types, both so that they will be prepared for other courses in their college careers and to develop their writing skills and strategies through practice with a range of assignments. In many first-year writing courses, for example, students begin with some sort of *personal*/narrative essay, usually one that requires them to describe, reflect on, and analyze some significant event or experience (see, e.g., Spack, 2006). The idea is that students who are becoming acclimated to college life in general and academic writing in particular can "warm up" to their environment by writing about a topic already familiar to them. Students are then usually asked to move on to *expository* writing, in which they articulate some sort of controlling idea or thesis and then provide support (explanation, definition, examples, argumentation, evidence, etc.) to develop that thesis. The most challenging forms of writing are usually *analytic* or *persuasive* essays in which students must state and defend an opinion or position on a topic.

These various tasks may or may not be text-based assignments, meaning that students must use assigned readings to generate ideas and support for their own writing. Even personal narrative assignments can be text-based, as some course readers include narratives written by professional writers for students to read and reflect on as they write their own narratives. Other common text-based assignments include *research* papers (which could include primary and/or secondary research information) and *literary analysis* papers, in which students respond in some way to a work(s) of fiction, poetry, or drama.

Another general model of writing task design incorporates so-called linked assignments, in which students pursue a specific topic over all or part of a term through the lenses of different task types. For example, students could write a factual report about a specific topic based on a source(s) they have examined. This task could be followed by another one in which students take a more critical stance toward the topic and by another in which additional sources of information are synthesized and the original discussion is expanded. Topics and sources for such tasks could be pre-selected for all students by the teacher (in what is often called a theme-based course, where all class readings and writing topics focus on a general topic, such as ecology or education or identity, and so forth) or individual students could choose and research their own topics.

A broader issue raised by this brief overview of task types is whether writing/ literacy courses are (or should be) for general purposes or whether they should be discipline-specific courses (e.g., writing in the sciences, legal writing, business writing, etc.). While there are passionate advocates of discipline-specific writing courses, others have cautioned that it can be difficult for English/writing instructors to attain the disciplinary knowledge needed to design and teach such courses, and that writing instructors' time is better spent helping students develop transferable linguistic knowledge (e.g., of academic vocabulary and specific syntactic structures), skills, strategies, and processes that can be utilized in a wide range of courses and assignments during their studies (see Spack, 1988). A number of U.S. universities have resolved this debate by having first-year courses be of a more general nature while sophomore or upper-division courses focus on writing in the disciplines or for specific purposes. Often these more advanced courses will be taught within the disciplinary departments themselves (rather than the English/writing department). For our purposes in this chapter, it is unlikely that an individual teacher will have decision-making authority as to whether his/her writing course is for general purposes or discipline-specific, but it is important to mention that this distinction exists and that the nature of the course will clearly influence or determine the types of tasks and content included in the writing course syllabus.

Topics

In addition to determining what types of writing students will do—which of course should also include consideration of informal writing assignments such as journal or blog entries, freewriting, timed in-class writing, and other homework or in-class exercises—the writing instructor must also determine the *topics or content* of the major reading and writing assignments. For L2 writers in particular, content issues include topics that will be interesting and engaging to the target audience and that will not pose unreasonable barriers due to unfamiliar language or cultural content. It has been suggested, for instance, that literary texts with antiquated language (such as Shakespeare) or with a strong regional/colloquial flavor (such as novels by Mark Twain) may not be appropriate for at least some L2 students (see Hedgcock & Ferris, 2009, for discussion).

A related topic/content issue is whether the teacher will prescribe all reading/ writing assignments or whether students will have some choice as to texts to read and topics to write about. While uniform texts and topics are easier for a teacher to work with—it is more straightforward to design classroom lessons and assessments if all students are doing the same thing—a certain degree of choice or autonomy can be engaging and empowering to students, and it provides the added benefit for the teacher of not having to read and respond to paper after paper with the exact same content.

Tasks and Topics for the Three Audiences

When we consider the characteristics of different L2 student audiences and the task/topic choices, several specific implications come to mind. First, international students, who likely have had little opportunity to write extended texts in English, may benefit the most from low-risk fluency-building tasks such as freewriting, journal entries, and so forth. Though some personal writing assignments might be uncomfortable to them culturally, if the tasks are sensitively designed, it may be easier initially for international students to write extended prose on personal experiences than to add the cognitive demands of expository, persuasive, or text-based tasks to the already formidable challenge of simply producing enough text in English. For instance, rather than asking students to reflect on "times they were treated unfairly" or "their most embarrassing experience," both of which may seem intrusive and face-losing to newly arrived students, they could describe their first impressions of college or of the new country and compare their current understanding of the context to their initial experience. The same generalization would likely hold for recently arrived resident students, who may have a bit more knowledge of the L2 culture but who also lack experience with writing extensively in English.

Second, students educated in their home countries and literate in their home languages may need and benefit from introduction to and explicit instruction about how to produce various English academic text types. Thus, general purposes expository and persuasive writing assignments may be important for them, especially if their own L1 has different conventions (Connor, 1996, 2003; Hinds, 1987; Kaplan, 1966). However, in selecting topics and supporting text materials, instructors need to take care that the content and language of the task will be accessible to these newcomers. For instance, a newly arrived international student who does not possess a driver's license and has never driven a car in the United States may not find a topic about laws against using cell phones while driving particularly interesting, while early-arriving students who have grown up in this society most likely have had firsthand experiences with and strong opinions about the issue.

A more subtle issue arises when students' cultural backgrounds influence their responses to a particular topic or prompt. For instance, students from socially conservative cultures might have strong negative opinions about women in the workplace, and their arguments might seem backward and unsophisticated to 21st-century American readers. A few years ago at my previous institution, a Writing Proficiency Examination (WPE) prompt asked students to critically assess the influence of the media on our society. Some ESL students, recent immigrants who had spent years in impoverished circumstances in their home countries, wrote responses along these lines: "I love the media. When I get up in the morning, I can turn on the Weather Channel or the Internet and find out what I should wear to school!" Coming from societies in which these everyday conveniences were unheard of, these students had a difficult time imagining any possible negative influences of the media—but this of course was far from the more complex analysis that the WPE readers expected from the student writers.

This discussion of task types is fairly typical as to both recommendations and current practices with regard to L2 literacy instruction, most or all of which has been based on an understanding of the traditional ESL student (primarily international students and late-arriving residents). However, the emergence of early-arriving L2 students in college-level writing instruction necessitates a careful look at task/topic issues with regard to the needs of this complex group. These early-arriving students tend to be lacking in strong L2 literacy skills in general and in academic literacy abilities in particular. Thus, they need instruction and practice in close reading of academic texts for comprehension and critical analysis and in specific academic writing skills, such as integration of sources, summary, paraphrase, citation, and quotation. While many college students of any language background also need assistance with these issues, among the L2 writers, early-arriving resident students may be the most lacking in these academic literacy skills. For example, in designing a class at UCLA especially for Generation 1.5 students, Holten (2002) decided that "it was more important for the . . . students to write consistently and frequently than to be bogged down with [a] heavy reading load" (p. 178); as a result, these students were required to read shorter texts than their mainstream counterparts in a first-year writing course (see Holten, 2002, Fig. 1, p. 179).

International students, in contrast, may have had experience with close reading and academic writing in their L1 (and maybe also in English), and due to earlier educational specialization in some countries, students may also be relatively comfortable with reading and writing about specialized academic topics in their major fields. In fact, international students at upper-division and graduate levels may function better in English when it is specialized and discipline-specific than in general education courses across various fields. In contrast, early-arriving students (and some late-arriving students) typically have a much stronger grasp of everyday English than academic English, and they may especially struggle with literacy requirements as they progress into upper-division or graduate major courses.

As to topics, it has been noted by scholars (e.g., Blanton, 1999; Harklau, Siegal, & Losey, 1999; Leki, 1992; Reid, 1998/2006b) focusing on early-arriving students that ESL classes in college tend to be aimed at the traditional (international/newcomers) population, with topics focusing on "first" and "new" experiences or on comparisons between their home country and the target country. Such topics would obviously not be appropriate for early-arriving students, who have little or no memory of the home country (Ferris & Hedgcock, 2005). In an effort to be more sensitive to a resident student audience, some teachers have chosen texts and topics related to the immigrant/minority experience (e.g., based on short young-adult novels such as *The House on Mango Street* or *Farewell to Manzanar* or *Children of the River*). Such topics, while probably better for resident students than ones designed for newly arrived international students, may also be problematic for early-arriving students, many of whom either view themselves primarily as Americans or have conflicting identities; these students may not view themselves as "immigrants" even though their parents are immigrants. Also, when such "immigrant/minority" literature is used, it runs the risk of alienating students whose cultural background is drastically different from that of the protagonist in the novel. Considering all of this, it may be best for teachers to focus in topic selection on issues of general human interest that transcend visa/immigration status or culture, such as friendship, family, work, education, current events, and so forth.

Materials Selection

Once instructors have set forth course goals and have a general sense of the types of tasks they will create for students, they can select textbooks and/or other materials to be used in the course.

Extensive Reading

In a literacy (reading/writing) course, particularly one that primarily focuses—as most college courses do—on writing, an instructor must consider carefully how much reading to assign students, both in and out of class. While this question circles back to needs analysis and course goals, it is also useful to observe that while early-arriving resident L2 students need instruction and practice in *intensive reading* strategies, students educated in other countries may additionally need teachers to facilitate their *extensive reading* (Aebersold & Field, 1997; Day & Bamford, 1998; Ferris & Hedgcock, 2005; Grabe & Stoller, 2002; Hedgcock & Ferris, 2009; Krashen, 2004; Seymour & Walsh, 2006). As previously noted, students learning English in other countries may have never been asked to read or write more than a page or two of English at a time and may find the reading load in American colleges and universities especially overwhelming. Further, due to their "eye" learner status and relatively limited exposure to the L2, they can benefit from the natural exposure to vocabulary, idioms, sentence patterns, and cultural information that extensive reading of authentic texts can provide. As many aspects of English cannot be taught at all, and others take years to acquire, extensive reading is the best "shortcut" to accelerated and advanced second language acquisition for time-pressed L2 college students (see Spack, 1997/2004 for an especially memorable example of this principle in her case study subject, "Yuko").

As discussed in L1/L2 work on extensive reading (e.g., Day & Bamford, 1998; Hedgcock & Ferris, 2009; Krashen, 2004; Seymour & Walsh, 2006), there are various ways in which the term is used in the literature and realized in the classroom. In its essence, *extensive reading* refers to "reading a great deal and with enjoyment." It is argued, especially by Krashen (2004), that the benefits of extensive reading primarily come from self-selected "free voluntary reading" (FVR), but there is evidence that teacher-assigned extensive reading also has positive effects on students' growth in vocabulary, grammar, spelling, reading comprehension, and writing skills (for reviews, see Day & Bamford, 1998; Krashen, 2004). Ideally, however, even when the teacher requires students to do a certain amount of extensive reading (e.g., a certain number of hours or pages per week or of books or articles per term), students will have some autonomy and choice as to what to read. Teachers should also facilitate extensive reading by helping students find appropriate materials and by providing some sort of structure or accountability, such as a reading log, reading groups, or book reports. More detailed suggestions for extensive reading can be found in Day and Bamford (1998), Hedgcock and Ferris (2009), and Seymour and Walsh (2006).

Textbooks, Handbooks, and Other Materials

It has been noted by L2 scholars that many commercially available reading/ writing textbooks are designed particularly for international "eye" learners as to topics and themes, scope of explanation about rhetorical patterns and modes (e.g., paragraph and essay structure), and the points at which grammatical explanations begin. For L2 audiences composed mainly of early-arriving students, some college instructors choose composition textbooks (readers, rhetorics, and handbooks) designed for mainstream (native speaker) courses and provide additional language support themselves through classroom instruction and individual feedback on student writing. Though there is a wide variety of options available to L2 reading/ writing teachers, awareness of the needs and characteristics of various student populations can help them to select texts most appropriate for the group of students they are serving. Figure 4.6 suggests some questions teachers can ask themselves to evaluate whether certain texts and support materials are a good fit for their students. This list, again, is not intended to be exhaustive; further, it is important to point out that most of the text characteristics could be helpful in some proportion or form to any L2 student audience. These questions simply help instructors to quickly look at the primary emphases of texts as an initial sorting tool. (See also Ferris & Hedgcock, 2005, Fig. 4.1, and Hedgcock & Ferris, 2009, Fig. 4.3, for detailed textbook evaluation forms that can be used or adapted for a more in-depth examination.)

As a final word on materials, extensive reading sources and commercial texts are obviously not the only resources used by teachers and their students, who today often turn to texts such as recent newspaper, magazine, and journal articles (either print or online versions) to read, discuss, and write about current issues and events or even to less traditional sources such as blogs, discussion boards, and social networking sites (e.g., Facebook or MySpace) for additional opportunities to read, write, interact with others, and encounter and experiment with language in a variety of ways. Teachers again need to use both commonsense evaluation criteria as well as awareness of students' background knowledge to assess the appropriateness of these additional sources for their students.

FIGURE 4.6

Textbook Evaluation Questions for the Three Audiences

Sample Characteristics	If Yes, Most Appropriate Audience(s)
Does the textbook provide information about and models of American academic paragraph and essay structure?	International and newly arrived immigrants
Do readings focus on experiences of "newcomers" and/or comparisons with home country/culture?	International
Does the text provide detailed instruction and practice in specific academic reading and writing strategies (e.g., annotating a text, summarizing, etc.)?	All
Do grammatical explanations (if any) assume prior knowledge of grammatical categories, terms, and rules?	International and "eye" learner recently arrived immigrants
Are writing tasks mainly focused on building overall writing fluency and confidence?	International
Does the text help students to develop and use more sophisticated academic language (vocabulary, syntax, cohesion)?	All

Specific Language Instruction

While developing accurate and effective language use, including vocabulary, sentence structure, mechanics, and cohesion within and between sentences and paragraphs is arguably important for all college students in writing courses, it is especially so for L2 students, who, as already noted, are generally even more likely to "produce less accurate and effective texts" (Hyland, 2002, p. 36) than their monolingual peers. In designing courses that include L2 college students, instructors must carefully consider how language-focused instruction (or what Holten, 2002, refers to as "the elephant in the room") fits into the big picture of the reading/composition class. Without such planning, instructors of L2 students may fall into one of three unhelpful patterns: (1) They may focus on grammar to excess, neglecting other important aspects of literacy instruction (see Truscott, 1996; Zamel, 1985); (2) They may neglect language issues altogether, preferring to focus on "higher-order concerns" and hoping that accuracy problems will "take care of themselves" or "fall into place" as students' general literacy processes and practices improve

(Eskey, 1983; Ferris, 1995; Horowitz, 1986; Zamel, 1982); or (3) They may address language haphazardly and unsystematically, "fitting in" grammar lessons or editing workshops or vocabulary development here and there on the rare occasions that time permits. None of these approaches are optimal, which is why a plan for addressing language should be in place when teachers are designing their courses.

Treatment of Error

Usually the most apparent and urgent language issue for classroom teachers of L2 writers is addressing errors that appear in student writing, both to help students improve their own self-editing skills (Bates, Lane, & Lange, 1993; Ferris, 1995, 2002, 2003, 2008; Lane & Lange, 1999) and to assist students in producing texts that meet the standards of acceptability for that particular course. As I have suggested elsewhere, *error treatment* in L2 writing includes at least three distinct concerns: (1) providing systematic and effective feedback to individual students; (2) providing grammar instruction and/or self-study resources to all students or to smaller groups of students with specific gaps in their knowledge; and (3) providing strategy training to student writers so that they can become better editors of their own work (Ferris, 1995, 2002, 2008; Ferris & Hedgcock, 2005). As already noted, the challenge lies primarily in deciding how to fit these error treatment components into an overall course plan. Figure 4.7 provides a sample scheme to address this logistical issue.

FIGURE 4.7
Sample Error Treatment Plan for a Writing Course Syllabus

A. General Activity Types
1. Begin each writing course with a diagnostic needs analysis.
2. In conjunction with teaching students about writing processes, include discussion of editing and introduce self-editing strategies.
3. Give students precise feedback on **individual error patterns** throughout the writing process. (This feedback could also include structured peer editing workshops.)
4. Give students time in class to self-edit marked texts and to chart their errors.
5. Design and deliver a series of mini-lessons on key grammar points and editing strategies.
6. Move students toward greater autonomy in finding and correcting their own errors.
B. Activities for Different Phases of the Course (assumes a 15-week semester)
Phase 1: Weeks 1–3: Focusing students on form
Phase 2: Weeks 4–10: Training students to recognize major error types
Phase 3: Weeks 11–15: Helping students to find and correct their own errors

Adapted from Ferris & Hedgcock, 2005, Fig. 7.8, p. 281, and pp. 287–288.

With regard to the needs of the different student audiences, these general error treatment suggestions will vary depending upon the make-up of the class. For example, diagnostic activities (Fig. 4.7, Part A.1) are especially important to assess the formal knowledge typically possessed by "eye" learners but not by "ear" learners. In a study on error feedback focused primarily on resident learners (including both recently arrived immigrants and Generation 1.5 students), it was found that the average student had only a tenuous grasp on basic grammatical rules and terms such as *verb, noun endings,* or *articles* (Ferris & Roberts, 2001). While "assume nothing" (with regard to students' prior knowledge of formal grammar) is probably good advice for any L2 writing instructor, it is particularly salient for those teaching mixed classes of international, late-arriving and early-arriving resident students and/or for those primarily teaching "ear" learners. This advice extends to issues such as individual feedback to students and the topics and approaches for grammar mini-lessons as well. These more specific classroom applications will be discussed in some detail in Chapter 5.

Academic Language Development

With L2 writers, the "eradication of errors" should not be instructors' only concern. L2 students at the college level also urgently need attention to:

- vocabulary development (for reading comprehension and for writing style: see Birch, 2007; Coxhead, 2000, 2006; Coxhead & Byrd, 2007; Conrad, 2008; Folse, 2004, 2008; Hedgcock & Ferris, 2009; Reid, 1998/2006b; Seymour & Walsh, 2006)

- intentional development of *strategic reading practices* in individual students (see Grabe & Stoller, 2002; see also Hedgcock & Ferris, 2009, and Seymour & Walsh, 2006)

- development of syntactic knowledge (especially for academic registers: see Byrd & Bunting, 2008; Conrad, 2008; Coxhead & Byrd, 2007; Reid, 1998/2006b; Seymour & Walsh, 2006; Schleppegrell, 2004; Schleppegrell & Colombi, 2002)

- understanding and using lexical and syntactic devices for cohesion and coherence within texts

It is not unusual for international students' texts to be simple and repetitive on the lexical level and to lack complexity and accuracy on the syntactic level as well (Hinkel, 2002; Hyland, 2002; Silva, 1993). Because of their relative lack of exposure to extended spoken and written input in the L2, they simply have not acquired an adequate linguistic repertoire (Byrd & Bunting, 2008; Conrad, 2008; Folse, 2008) and/or they may not have the confidence to use more academic vocabulary and syntax because they are trying to avoid errors (see the classic treatment of this topic by Schachter, 1974; see also Truscott, 2007). Early- and late-arriving resident L2 students also lack an adequate academic vocabulary, but the gaps manifest themselves in different ways (and occur for different reasons). Consider the following text excerpt from an early-arriving L2 student in a college ESL writing course:

> A new life style meant new friends, new home, back with my family, but most importantly a new language. I never thought how difficult it would be to learn a new language. Spanish is my first language, and soon after, English became my second language. Have **you** ever been *place* in a class room **were** the teacher spoke only English? **Well,** if I ever have to answer that question, I am sure **you** would know the answer. In high school, I was once placed in a room with native English speakers and sometimes I found myself lost, trying to figure out what they were trying to say. Communication was a barrier. Every time I would *leaved* the classroom my brain was full of thoughts, but unable to *delivered* them because my English was not very good. It was the worst *feelings* **ever** because I felt alienated, unwanted, not *welcoming*, and at times it felt like if I was not as important as the other students.

This text[2] is interesting because it includes typical ESL errors (in *italics*) such as verb tense and form issues as well as typical early-arrival issues (in **bold**) such as inappropriate use of the second person and informal language such as *Well* to start a sentence. While early-arriving students and other resident "ear" learners may be more fluent and have a more developed everyday vocabulary than their newcomer counterparts, as discussed in Chapter 2, the vocabulary they have acquired may not be appropriate or adequate for academic settings.

With these issues in mind, a teacher of L2 readers/writers in course planning should consider how to incorporate instruction and practice in vocabulary development in general and specifically how to help students achieve more lexical and syntactic variety while still staying within an appropriate register for academic discourse. Again, it can be challenging to envision how to fit these concerns into a busy composition/reading course syllabus, but it is important that teachers do so. Ideally, such discussions could be integrated in conjunction with reading activities (analyzing the vocabulary and style used by other authors) and with writing activities (looking over already composed drafts to see where vocabulary, syntax, and cohesion could be improved). Additional specific suggestions are discussed in Chapter 5. In short, the teacher of L2 writers must take seriously the need to work with students on language development throughout a term—and thoughtful planning from the outset about how and when to approach language issues in the course is an absolutely critical part of course design.

Classroom Assessment and Grading Practices

A final issue to consider in planning a course for L2 readers/writers is how progress will be assessed. Generally speaking, course goals (above) should be directly tied to assessment schemes: How will the teacher know that goals have been met? In a writing course, assessment can be formal (e.g., through out-of-class revised essays or portfolios, in-class timed writing, reading, grammar, or vocabulary quizzes) or informal (e.g., through class participation in workshop activities, extensive reading logs, writing journal entries, etc.). (See Ferris & Hedgcock, 2005, Ch. 8 and Hedgcock & Ferris, 2009, Ch. 9 for a detailed discussion of classroom reading and writing assessment for L2 students; see Chapter 3 of this volume for further discussion of assessment.)

With regard to diverse student audiences, while timed writing is arguably problematic for all students and especially for L2 students (see discussion in Chapter 3), it is particularly difficult for international students, for whom fluency in language use (both speaking and writing) is a daunting challenge, especially under stress and time pressure. On the other hand, as most recently arrived students may have had limited experience with process approach strategies, the development of skills in planning, revision, collaboration, and editing can be facilitated by a portfolio grading scheme, which privileges process. Finally, for "eye" learners educated in their home countries, graded assignments requiring extensive reading may be extremely important. (See Day & Bamford, 1998 and Hedgcock & Ferris, 2009, for detailed suggestions about possible assessment approaches for extensive reading.)

As already noted, early-arriving L2 students may already be familiar with process approach techniques, may be fairly fluent (relative to L2 newcomers), and may have been taught "typical" American academic paragraph and essay patterns in their secondary English classes. However, they have a strong need to develop specific academic reading and writing skills (see Chapter 2), so perhaps a portion of the class grading scheme could be comprised of reading/writing analysis activities and quizzes as well as measurable progress in using more academic and less informal language in their own writing. While "ear" learners can undoubtedly also benefit from extensive reading assignments, perhaps more important for them is the ability to comprehend, analyze, and critically discuss academic texts through intensive reading activities, and classroom assessment schemes should help students to build and demonstrate these skills. To summarize, assessment or grading schemes should help to operationalize the course goals, which in turn should be carefully selected based on a thoughtful and thorough needs analysis. Thus the course design process, while described in a linear fashion in this chapter, is truly interconnected and recursive.

Considerations for "Mixed" (Mainstream and Multilingual) Classes

The previous discussion has been aimed at L2 teachers designing courses for ESL/multilingual audiences. However, as noted in Chapter 3, multilingual students of all descriptions are increasingly found in mainstream composition courses in addition to courses in the disciplines. Course planning, as well as day-to-day instruction, is challenging for these instructors, who must balance the needs of mainstream students with the needs of an increasingly diverse multilingual audience. It is probably safe to say that most mainstream students could also benefit from the types of academic reading/writing analysis activities suggested for early-arriving students; teachers whose classes include members of this L2 audience may not need to adjust classroom instruction (as to goals, tasks, topics, and materials) much, but they will need to consider how to address the complex language needs (which, as in the student text example above, can include ESL features in their texts) of the multilingual students in the class. Assuming that extensive language development work during class would not be appropriate in such settings, alternatives for teachers can include extra individual attention for students with specialized language needs and/or identifying useful on-campus support mechanisms, such as one-to-one tutoring, adjunct tutorials, and so forth.

Specific Considerations for International Students

Mainstream instructors whose classes include international students will further need to consider cultural knowledge embedded in assigned texts and tasks and perhaps provide additional support in the form of background information about the text for newcomers. Teachers should also be aware of contrasting organizational patterns (possibly entailing the need for instruction on paragraph and essay organization options) and the international students' relative unfamiliarity (and possible discomfort) with typical composition class activities such as peer response and multiple drafting. As noted, in course design teachers will need to take into account their students' lack of experience with reading lengthy texts in English as they decide what kinds of reading materials to include. Finally, instructors will need to consider in their grading scheme whether international students' lack of fluency (i.e., shorter texts) and lack of variety in vocabulary and syntax will be "held against them" and/or whether they can/should provide additional input to students about these issues in an effort to help them develop a more sophisticated academic writing style. As many U.S. colleges and universities mainstream all L2 students, even international students, at the college level (i.e., first-year or freshman writing) (Braine, 1996; Costino & Hyon, 2007; Matsuda & Silva, 1999), all writing instructors need to be aware of these competing needs and complex issues as they plan and teach their courses.

This chapter reviewed six steps or sub-topics related to the complex endeavor of course design for multiple L2 student audiences. Though most of the suggestions in this chapter are not new, the challenging question for individual teachers becomes *balance* and *proportion*. For example, while all students can benefit from *both* intensive and extensive reading activities, given limited time and resources in any specific setting, teachers may choose to privilege one over the other as to class/homework time spent and relative weighting in the grading scheme. Similarly, all students need to work on academic writing sub-skills, effective writing process strategies, and language development (both as to accuracy and variety)—but the amount and types of these skills and activities may vary in a given class depending on the characteristics of the target audience. Further, when international, late-arriving resident and early-arriving resident students are found in classes together in roughly equivalent proportions, a teacher may need to design instruction and assessment differently *within the same class* to better meet the differing needs of the various groups of students in the class. Even if teachers are unable or unwilling to make changes in global course design, their sensitivity and creativity with regard to the questions raised in this chapter (see Fig. 4.1) will lead to better outcomes for individual students. While the issues can be arduous to sort through, as we begin to develop a deeper understanding of the fact that "there is no such thing as a generalized ESL student" (Raimes, 1991, p. 420), it is critical that all instructors of L2 writers move away from the types of stereotypes articulated from my own experience at the beginning of this chapter and toward a specialized, thoughtful approach to the unique needs of every group of L2 students they encounter. In course design for the three L2 audiences defined in this volume, truly one size does not fit all.

QUESTIONS FOR REFLECTION AND DISCUSSION

1. Figure 4.2 provides an extensive list of needs analysis questions to consider in course planning. Were you surprised by any of these? Are there others you could add?

2. In the section on goals, it is suggested that some students may benefit in the earlier stages of their academic writing development from a structured presentation of paragraph and essay development (based on the "paragraph-pattern" composition teaching approach). This is a controversial point, as some researchers and teachers believe strongly that presenting students with a "formula" for writing is always counterproductive. What is your view on this issue?

3. This chapter argues strongly that a thoughtful and systematic approach to error treatment and academic language development is an indispensable part of course planning when some or all of the students are L2 writers. Do you agree with this stance? Do you see any problems or dangers with it?

4. In the materials selection section, it is suggested that in classes with mixed audiences, topics and texts that focus on issues of universal interest rather than newcomer or immigrant experiences may be preferable. What is your view of this advice? If possible, survey a few L2 composition textbooks, looking at tasks and topics. Do any of these books seem "skewed" toward one target audience or another?

5. If possible, examine several composition syllabi aimed at L2 student audiences (either for an ESL composition course or a mixed L1/L2 writing course). Using the questions in the chart in Fig. 4.1 as a framework, see if you can identify the teacher's approach to the various issues raised in this chapter (or lack of consideration of particular issues).

CHAPTER ENDNOTES

[1] I am well aware from my own experience and the anecdotes (or horror stories) of others, that these "optimal" course design conditions are not always in place: Teachers are hired at the last minute, handed a textbook or syllabus and told what/how to teach, or they volunteer for or are thrust into instructional settings for which they have not been trained. Nonetheless, even under these less ideal circumstances, teachers should, to the degree possible, always be thinking through the various course-planning steps presented in this chapter.

[2] I am grateful to my former student, Brigitte Rabie, for providing this text excerpt.

Chapter 5

Different L2 Audiences and Considerations for Classroom Instruction

The most efficient way to teach English is to provide direct instruction with clear explanations, expose students to the language features being taught, provide students with multiple opportunities to practice the features, and give supportive instructional feedback.

—Scarcella, 2003, p. 10

CHAPTERS 3 AND 4 EXAMINED BIG-PICTURE ISSUES related to program development and course design with regard to the different L2 student audiences identified in this volume. Chapter 5 turns to day-to-day classroom instruction and examines specific issues and techniques that may help teachers best meet the needs of the diverse student groups co-existing in their post-secondary language/literacy courses.

Entire books have been written on various subtopics that could be covered in this chapter on teaching reading, writing, grammar, vocabulary, and listening/speaking skills to L2 students in various settings, so there is no attempt here to be comprehensive in coverage.[1] Rather, we will focus on several sub-topics that have arisen in the discussion thus far as being salient to consider not only for all L2 students but across *different groups* of L2 students. In particular, we will examine:

- interaction issues in and out of class: teacher and students; students with each other
- approaches to academic language development: teaching academic grammar and vocabulary
- developing effective reading and writing strategies and processes
- providing and/or facilitating feedback on writing
- providing and/or facilitating or identifying additional support inside and outside of class for varying student needs

As in Chapter 4, we also state several assumptions on which the discussion rests: (1) students have already been placed into classes using programmatic placement mechanisms (see Chapter 3); (2) teachers have been diligent in performing needs analyses and have identified course goals; outlined major tasks, topics, and assignments; and selected or identified materials for intensive and extensive reading (see Chapter 4); and (3) teachers have begun their courses with activities and assessments (e.g., questionnaires, discussions, reading and writing samples, or tests) designed to help them get to know their students and individual/group strengths and weaknesses. Finally, although most of this chapter focuses on instructional practices within ESL reading/writing courses, we end the discussion with considerations for mainstream courses that include multilingual students along with monolingual native English speakers.

Interaction Patterns

Overview of Issues

Chapter 4 began with a narrative about how my own understanding of and assumptions about working with English L2 students have changed over a 25-year teaching career. For instance, in my early years of teaching I worked with a traditional population of newly arrived international students and adult immigrants. In most cases, their aural/oral skills were not as developed as their reading/writing skills, so classroom and one-to-one interaction between the students and me was challenging. As a new ESL teacher, I was intentional about modifying my speech: talking more slowly; enunciating more carefully; avoiding slang and idioms; explaining problematic words and phrases as they arose; and using repetition, redundancy, and extralinguistic information (facial expressions, tone of voice, gestures, visuals such as pictures and realia) to ensure or at least improve student comprehension. However, in recent years as I have worked with a primarily early-arriving resident L2 audience, I have transitioned to speaking to those students just as I speak to my other (non-ESL) classes, with no slowing of pace, exaggerated articulation and emphases, or avoidance of cultural-specific slang and idioms. This shift was not a conscious one as it occurred, but it reflects my awareness of the students' greater aural/oral proficiency, cultural knowledge, and comfort with "typical" interactions found in American classrooms. However, as these classes also usually include a few international students, I still need to be aware that their experience and comfort level is not the same as that of their more assimilated classmates and take steps to make sure they are not becoming lost and that they feel included in the classroom community.

Research on academic oral skills has not been as abundant as research on academic literacy skills, and little to none of it has differentiated among various audiences of L2 students.[2] To summarize, researchers have found that:

- listening comprehension is challenging for L2 students in academic settings (Flowerdew, 1994), but the addition of various types of visuals and other support materials (e.g., lecture notes or podcasts on the Internet) makes formal lecture comprehension somewhat easier than previously. On the other hand, informal class discussions, in which comments and questions flow freely from instructor to students, from students to instructor, and from students to one another, pose formidable challenges especially for students who are newcomers (Ferris & Tagg, 1996a; Ferris, 1998; Lynch, 1994; Mason, 1994).

• L2 students in classes with monolingual native English speakers may be hesitant to speak up during class discussions due to cultural influences or insecurity about their own oral skills (Belcher, 1999; Ferris & Tagg, 1996a; Ferris, 1998).

• L2 students may have difficulty interacting with or asking questions of the instructor both in and out of class (Scarcella, 2003).

To these basic generalizations about challenges L2 students face with regard in classroom interaction can be added the discomfort and/or resentment that early-arriving residents (those who have been in the English-speaking environment for some years) are reported to feel about being placed in ESL classes with newcomers (Chiang & Schmida, 1999; Costino & Hyon, 2007; Harklau et al., 1999; Ortmeier-Hooper, 2008) and the assumption that newcomers may feel just as uncomfortable with these students, whom they perceive as being fluent in English and fully acculturated, as they do with "mainstream" monolingual native English speakers. With these admittedly limited generalizations and assumptions in mind, we turn to implications and suggestions for the teacher attempting to serve different L2 audiences in the same class.

Teacher-Student Classroom Interactions

If the class is "mixed" (meaning that it includes L2 students from two or all three different audiences) teachers may need to strive for a balance between the extremes of excessive modification of classroom speech and none at all. Early- and late-arriving resident students students with a few years of experience in the U.S. educational system will notice and resent being addressed as if they were newcomers and new to studying in the English language, but students with less experience in English-speaking classrooms will likely be left behind if no adjustments are made. Teachers could slow their pace somewhat to accommodate the new arrivals and provide extra support in the forms of visuals (handouts, slides, etc.) and additional materials on a course website such as lecture notes, audio versions of lectures and discussions, and other resources like glossaries of key terms or comprehension questions. As already noted, today's classroom technology provides many options to help learners preview or review material presented in class.

As previously mentioned, one typical modification that ESL teachers make is to avoid cultural references, idioms, and slang, opting for more accessible basic vocabulary. In a mixed class, teachers may still wish to minimize the use of such forms, but to the extent they occur in teacher talk or in open class discussion, the teacher could use the more assimilated students as informants, asking them to explain, define, or illustrate words or phrases that arise in discussion or in texts the class is reading.

A final consideration in teacher-student class interaction is how students gain the floor to ask questions or make comments. Although most U.S. teachers welcome student questions or comments, they tend to expect students to initiate them. Many ESL teachers perform frequent comprehension checks during class presentations ("Any questions?" "Do you understand?" "Does everyone know what _____ means?"). The problem, however, is that many students raised and educated in other cultures are too polite and/or too concerned with losing face to ask questions or to admit that they do not understand what they have heard (Ferris, 1998; Ferris & Tagg, 1996b; Scarcella, 2003). Doing so in their minds not only publicly showcases their own shortcomings but implicitly criticizes the teacher for being unclear. Such concerns are no doubt exacerbated by being among peers who are much more confident and experienced with the language and the educational setting than these newcomers are. In this regard, an ESL class that includes early-arriving L2 students might feel just as threatening to traditional newcomers as would a mainstream class with monolingual English speakers. The differences among those peers (e.g., the gaps that some late- and early-arriving residents possess in academic reading and writing) would be more apparent to the teacher than to the students themselves. Teachers thus must provide more structure if they expect all of their students to ask questions for clarification, make comments, or otherwise participate in class discussions. For instance, they might provide a few minutes at the end of a class session or at a transition point during a lesson for students to respond privately in writing to specific questions (to check comprehension) or to do a quickwrite about what they just learned and what their opinion or reaction to it is. Another (probably riskier) option is to pose questions orally and to call on various students to respond; students can also review material (points on an outline, key terms, etc.) in pairs or small groups in which they can help each other.

An additional option is to use online class discussion formats (Belcher, 1999) in which the teacher can pose questions, following a class presentation, through which students can demonstrate understanding of material (and perhaps further analysis and application), ask questions, make comments, and so forth. The unique public/private format of such discussions allows less confident students to speak up (without the pressures of seizing the floor in a class discussion, interrupting a lecture to ask questions, or formulating an accurate and well articulated question or comment under time pressure) and to benefit from receiving replies from classmates as well as reading their posts in a more relaxed environment. Figure 5.1 shows such an example of such an online prompt, given after a class meeting and discussion of assigned reading in a master's-level TESOL class on L2 reading, so that students could reflect on and respond to the material (and read and comment on each other's posts, as well). The content of this particular prompt

---

FIGURE 5.1
Sample Online Discussion Prompt

Reflect on our discussion and activities on "the reader" in class this week. Think about what you learned about:

- yourself as a reader
- the complexities and challenges of being an L2 reader
- the types of information a teacher of L2 readers needs to collect and consider in planning instruction, selecting materials, and teaching lessons

Write 1–2 paragraphs of narrative (not bullet points) in response to the prompt above. You may focus on what you personally thought was most interesting, important, and enlightening—no need to simply summarize or even comment on all three "bullets" above.

Begin your post with one quotation from Chapter 2 (include the page number) that best informs or illustrates your own thoughts in the post.

---

is specific to the course, but it could be easily adapted for many different courses or topics.

Teacher-Student Out-of-Class Interactions

One issue raised in the literature is the unwillingness of L2 students (particularly recent arrivals) to ask the instructor for assistance outside of class. For newcomers, this may well be due to cultural differences regarding teacher-student interactions and differing prior educational experiences, but even early-arriving resident students may have little experience with such interactions if their secondary experience was relatively sheltered from mainstream coursework. All students can therefore benefit from the teacher's explicit invitation to ask questions via email or to make a visit during office hours. Depending on the time and space available, some teachers may wish to schedule and require individual conferences with their students as part of the course syllabus. However, teachers should be aware that students from some cultural backgrounds are extremely uncomfortable with such one-to-one interactions, so they might consider a two-to-one (two students at a time) conference instead (Ferris, 2003; Ferris & Hedgcock, 2005). Further, for all students, it can be helpful to discuss in class before conferences are held what the purposes and expectations are and perhaps ask students to write up and bring in specific questions or materials that will be the focus of conversation during conferences (e.g., summary of a reading or outline or draft of an essay). Finally, this discussion about online posts highlights another tool for teacher-student interaction, as the instructor and can read and comment on individual posts and thus pursue a dialogue with a particular student (even one who would not take initiative to email or visit the instructor).

Student-Student Interactions

Teachers must also consider how they will facilitate work done in and out of class among peers, such as pair and group work in class, peer review of student papers outside of class, and group projects that might require additional collaboration outside of class. Teachers of traditional ESL students (i.e., international students and late-arriving residents) have expressed concerns about students' desire to work with students from their own L1 background and their subsequent tendency to not converse in English. Such students may be uncomfortable, from both a cultural and linguistic standpoint, with peer interactions with L2 classmates who are "different," either because of their L1/cultural background or because those classmates appear more acculturated than they themselves are. On the other hand, late-arriving and early-arriving resident students might be frustrated with being asked to work with peers whose oral language skills are not as strong as their own and who seem very different with regard to cultural knowledge and life experience.

It is important for teachers to know who their students are and to anticipate those issues. With some forethought, a teacher can create a strength from what initially appears to be a problem. For example, the teacher can pair or group students so that each member of the group brings different strengths, such as formal grammar knowledge, strong L2 reading/vocabulary skills, background knowledge about the target culture, and so forth. Tasks can then be structured so that different group members can contribute equally. For instance, if students are discussing an assigned reading in a small group, perhaps they could be asked to define specific culture-specific or idiomatic terms (a task that would play to the strengths of early-arriving students) but also ask them to complete a grammar-focused task such as tracing verb tense usage in the text, a task that highlights the formal knowledge of the "eye" learners. In addition, the teacher should look for opportunities to build classroom community based on celebrating differences (such as having students share something interesting about their unique backgrounds) and recognizing shared struggles (grappling with the demands of the L2 and feelings about being a minority or a newcomer in the target culture). While meeting the needs of mixed classes is challenging, sensitive and creative teachers can forestall many problems and even create enriching learning opportunities as long as they are aware of the issues and the possibilities.

Academic Language Development

Chapter 4 noted that one of the key issues that an L2 teacher must face in designing courses is how to address students' language issues. While many teachers would prefer instead to present content, model and facilitate writing processes, and teach reading strategies, research in various aspects of second language acquisition is quite consistent in demonstrating that students need both formal *instruction* in academic language (vocabulary and grammar) and *feedback* about the ways in which their own production (particularly in writing) falls short of acceptable standards for academic discourse.[3]

Vocabulary Knowledge

Chapter 2 noted that vocabulary issues are extremely significant, not only for SLA in general but for academic literacy in particular. For L2 students grappling with reading and writing texts at the college level, they must cope with at least three distinct levels of vocabulary knowledge: (1) general everyday vocabulary; (2) general academic vocabulary (Coxhead, 2000, 2006); and (3) specialized vocabulary related to particular disciplines, not only in their own major field but, in the case of undergraduates, in general education courses and perhaps minor fields. It is estimated that the typical monolingual native English speaker completing the twelfth grade possesses a vocabulary upward of 40,000 words (Coxhead, 2006; Folse, 2004; Nation, 2001; Scarcella, 2003). Most L2 students, regardless of background, cannot approach that vocabulary size. While early-arriving students especially may be very proficient with regard to everyday vocabulary in English, they tend to be lacking in academic vocabulary knowledge, a deficit that manifests itself both in reading comprehension and in writing, where their lexical choices are often overly conversational and informal for academic discourse (such as in the text excerpt shown in Chapter 4). These students need to be informed first about the register differences that exist and then about choices they can and should make in their own texts to make their writing more sophisticated and appropriate for its target audience.

In contrast, students educated in their own L1 may possess academic vocabulary knowledge (in L1 or to a lesser degree in English) and may also have specialized knowledge of particular fields, as some educational systems begin disciplinary specialization even at the secondary level, and/or they may have done college-level work in their home countries. However, their general vocabulary knowledge will still be much less than that of both monolingual students and early-arriving L2 students, and such knowledge is important in understanding new vocabulary in context when it is heard in a class lecture or encountered in a textbook (Coxhead, 2006; Folse, 2004). Also, they may be aware of academic registers but not proficient enough in English overall to utilize academic or specialized vocabulary accurately in written discourse, producing "thesaurus errors" by using words or phrases inappropriate for a specific context or by failing to make syntactic adjustments required by the substitution of a synonym. Take this example from an international student text: *I kept myself **concentrated on** my studies.* Contrast this inaccurate rendition with the lexical paraphrase: *I kept myself **focused on** my studies.* We can also use the phrasal verbs *concentrated on* and *focused on* synonymously in other constructions, such as *I concentrated/focused on my studies.* The only time the two phrases cannot be interchangeable is in the reflexive (*kept myself*) construction. However, this is a fairly fine syntactic point, and it is not surprising that an international student writer such as this one would reason that (a) using synonyms for variety makes texts more interesting and sophisticated and (b) *focus on* and *concentrate on* are phrases that can be used synonymously, so the construction should be allowable. (Another similar error is *emphasize on;* contrast this with the acceptable *(place) emphasis on.)* On the other hand, a monolingual native English speaker or even an orally fluent early-arriving L2 student would be less likely to make such an error, as those students' more highly developed intuitions would tell them that it "sounds wrong," even if they cannot explain *why* it is wrong.

It is beyond the scope of this chapter or volume to discuss vocabulary instruction in depth, so several teaching suggestions relevant to the varying student audiences under consideration and the relevant issues are presented. These are summarized in Figure 5.2 and discussed further.

Using Word Lists to Explain Register Differences

L2 readers and writers in academic settings are well aware that they lack an adequate English vocabulary. It may thus be enlightening to them to learn that there are different general types of vocabulary and that certain words tend to occur frequently or infrequently in different types of texts. For example, early-arriving L2 students who graduated from U.S. high schools may be interested to hear that the words on the Academic Word List (AWL) (Coxhead, 2000, 2006) are only rarely found in fiction (which they probably read for high school English classes) (Coxhead & Byrd, 2007). This may help them understand why they struggle to understand their college texts despite longstanding (or even lifelong) residence

---

FIGURE 5.2
Academic Vocabulary Development for the Three Audiences

1. Explain the different types/registers of vocabulary found in academic discourse, using illustrations from word lists.

2. Teach students strategies for analyzing problematic vocabulary in course texts and in other texts they encounter in school.

3. Encourage or require students to supplement class instruction with self-directed vocabulary learning.

4. Discuss the importance of lexical variety and appropriate register choices in academic writing. Also raise student awareness about collocations and syntactic consequences of using synonyms.

5. Help students review their own writing to analyze and revise their vocabulary choices to improve accuracy, variety, and sophistication.

---

in an English-speaking country. Similarly, international students may also have read literary texts in their English courses in their home countries and newspaper articles in preparatory ESL classes in the United States, and neither group of texts utilizes AWL items frequently. Further, as noted by Coxhead and Byrd (2007), "academic" words such as *notwithstanding* and *paradigm* are also unlikely to be heard in everyday conversation.

Teachers can show students samples of the General Service List and the AWL so that they can get a sense of the differences and begin to understand how synonymous words and phrases may be inappropriate when used in various registers (e.g., the distinction between *find out* and *investigate*). L2 students who are newcomers to the United States may also especially appreciate the Vocabulary Profiler tool on the *The Compleat Lexical Tutor* (Cobb, 2007, http://lextutor.ca), which analyzes texts into General Service Lists (most frequent 1,000 and 2,000 words in English texts), the AWL, and off-list words, which tend to include proper names, slang, and culture-specific references. Off-list items in a text may be a signal to these students and their teachers that further explanation or background may be needed (see also Hedgcock & Ferris, 2009, Chapters 3, 5, and 8, for a discussion of how this free online tool may be used in text selection and instructional prioritizing; see Coxhead & Byrd, 2007).

Teaching Strategies for Word Analysis in Academic Reading

L2 students have two separate but related problems in coping with academic vocabulary demands. First, they must learn to predict, analyze, and investigate meanings of unfamiliar words and phrases they encounter in their assigned reading. Second, they must utilize a general academic vocabulary and content-specific vocabulary in their own writing. While the first task is larger—most people's receptive or passive vocabularies are larger than their productive or active vocabularies—the second may be more difficult, as it requires complex knowledge and decision-making. Students can be taught to use the context to predict meanings of words, to use knowledge of English morphology (roots and affixes) for intraword analysis (see Birch, 2007; Hedgcock & Ferris, 2009; Koda, 2004), and to accurately and efficiently use dictionaries and other resources to investigate new words or alternate meanings where context and morphological analyses fall short. Students should be given opportunities to apply these skills not only to texts used in the language/literacy course but also to academic texts used in other courses so that they can see how textual information, prior linguistic knowledge, and extra-textual resources can be used to address lexical gaps while reading.

Coxhead and Byrd (2007) make the additional point that in order to help students develop and practice strategies for analyzing vocabulary in academic texts, teachers must select authentic samples of academic discourse for students to read—that is, they must go beyond the literary and journalistic selections found in many ESL reading textbooks and ask students to read texts such as chapters from college textbooks, journal articles, lab reports, and so forth (see Seymour & Walsh, 2006, among others, for a further discussion of this point). In addition, students must read such texts not merely for content but for language analysis practice:

> By working with texts of authentic length and language, students can learn strategies for recognizing, dealing with, and then using the new words that they find in required reading materials. Thus, the work with academic reading passages should not focus exclusively on the content of the reading but also include study of the academic language, along with work on strategies for vocabulary learning. (Coxhead & Byrd, 2007, p. 133)

The necessity for and appropriateness of these activity types may well vary according to the type(s) of student audiences being considered in a particular setting. For example, students who are literate and educated in their L1 and whose L1 is quite different from English with regard to morphology may be both less aware of the ways in which English word meaning can sometimes (but not always) be deconstructed through morphological analysis *and* less familiar with English inflectional and derivational affixes and their purposes and with common English roots and their meanings (Birch, 2007; Hedgcock & Ferris, 2009; Koda, 2004). Thus, such students may benefit more than other groups from direct instruction about morphology and intra-word analysis skills. On the other hand, "eye" learners who have studied English extensively in a classroom may be more familiar with the utility of a good dictionary while reading than "ear" learners who have picked up most of what they know about English from their surroundings. Late-arriving and early-arriving L2 residents may therefore benefit from a formal introduction to the types of information contained in a dictionary and how to identify correct word/phrase meanings in a text given a list of alternate possibilities in the dictionary (see Folse, 2004, and Coxhead, 2006, for sample activities). Finally, while all L2 readers can benefit from exercises to predict word meanings from the larger context, it is important for teachers to realize that L2 students' ability to do so may be more limited than that of native English speakers, as there may be other elements of the text (syntax, morphology, content) in addition to the unfamiliar lexical item that are also unfamiliar to English learners. In other words, "guessing word meanings from context" is only helpful insofar as the surrounding context is helpful, transparent, and not otherwise confusing to the reader (Folse, 2004), so while it is a useful strategy, it may be more limited than we had previously realized, especially for L2 students, and students need to use it in combination with other information.

Encourage or Require Self-Directed Vocabulary Learning

Current L2 vocabulary researchers appear to be consistent in arguing that some direct instruction on vocabulary (both specific lexical items and learning strategies) is necessary and appropriate (Coxhead, 2006; Folse, 2004; Grabe & Stoller, 2002; Nation, 2001; Seymour & Walsh, 2006). In addition, most recommend that students be taught to identify, analyze, and record new vocabulary that they encounter, particularly in assigned course readings. Various techniques for approaching such self-directed learning have been suggested (see Folse, 2004, for one), including vocabulary logs or notebooks and individual vocabulary note cards, and they include common characteristics: Students list the word in the context in which they encountered it, research it using the dictionary (to find definition[s], word families, collocations, etc.), and attempt to use the word in new sentences of their own. The notebook or cards enable review (and give the teacher something to grade).

The possible drawback to this approach is that students may or may not self-identify words that are especially relevant to their future endeavors but rather may focus on items that are obscure and/or unique to a particular text, rather than frequent or academic vocabulary. On the other hand, training students to identify, analyze, and learn new vocabulary and holding them accountable in some way for doing so teaches them good habits and strategies that may serve them well in their future studies. In particular, a self-directed vocabulary learning program is an important supplement in an L2 class in which students' diverse experiences in learning English will have resulted in different lexical knowledge bases (and resulting gaps in vocabulary). Figure 5.3 shows a sample self-directed vocabulary learning tool. Both Coxhead and Folse suggest that vocabulary notebooks leave additional room on each page so that learners can record additional examples they come across and make further notes. Finally, Coxhead (2006) offers this further caveat or warning:

> One reason why some learners have been unsuccessful with recording words is they have spent a lot of time transferring information from a dictionary directly onto the page. These learners did not process the information in a meaningful way or try to use the words in their speaking or writing. (p. 68)

FIGURE 5.3

Sample Vocabulary Notebook

Word or Phrase	Brief Example	Grammatical Category	Word Family Members	Collocations	Meaning	Your Own Sentence

Adapted from Coxhead, 2006, and Folse, 2004.

Raise Awareness about Lexical and Syntactic Variety in Academic Writing

As noted in Chapter 2, L2 writing can be "marked" or "accented" by a lack of variety, leaving an impression of unsophisticated, underdeveloped writing even if the text is virtually error-free (e.g., Hinkel, 2002; Hyland, 2002; Silva, 1993). The sample text (page 42) written by John, an international student, illustrates this issue. Depending on their prior experiences with English writing, students may have encountered one of three approaches to instruction:

1. Neglect of lexical/syntactic variety issues, either because the teacher was unaware of how to approach the topic or because the teacher and students were more focused on avoiding errors (leading to simple, "safe" lexical and syntactic choices) than on developing a mature writing style.

2. A mechanical approach to instruction that included sentence-combining drills and teaching of lists of "set" transitional words and phrases to plug into texts at appropriate points to achieve cohesion. This approach, while it may effectively communicate to students the need to vary their writing choices, tends to fall short of building true writing competence and may in fact lead to errors (out-of-control sentences and incorrectly applied transitions).

3. An overemphasis on using dictionaries and thesauruses to promote lexical variety without a complete understanding of syntactic and register implications of using synonyms, leading students to find synonyms and use them inappropriately (from a grammatical or sociolinguistic standpoint) in their texts.

A more effective approach to the issue of lexical/syntactic variety in academic writing would include several elements:

- explicit presentation of lexical items and syntactic structures useful for general academic purposes and in specific disciplines, where appropriate (see Byrd & Bunting, 2008; Conrad, 2008; Coxhead, 2006; Coxhead & Byrd, 2007; Folse, 2008; Reid, 2006a; Seymour & Walsh, 2006)

- analysis of how lexical and syntactic variety and cohesion are achieved in authentic texts across various genres (going well beyond decontextualized sentence-combining or lists of transitions)

- explanation of possible issues or problems raised by synonym use, analysis of errors, and practice with alternatives

- classroom instruction and practice in paraphrasing and summarizing ideas from other authors' texts (see Folse, 2008; Schuemann, 2008)

*Teach Students to Review Their Own Writing to Improve Lexical
Accuracy, Variety, and Sophistication*

In the same way that writing teachers should teach students self-editing strategies to identify and address lexical, morphological, syntactic, and mechanical problems or errors in their texts (e.g., noun plurals, articles, verb tenses, prepositions, subject-verb agreement, etc.), students can learn to look critically at their own texts during the revision and editing phases, when content and organization are more or less established, to find ways to improve the lexical and syntactic style and cohesion of their texts. Teachers could, for example, present a mini-lesson on lexical variety, ask students to look through their own texts for key, repeated words, and then discuss ways they could effectively vary their word choice. Students could practice making some wording changes and check them immediately with a partner and/or a teacher to ensure that the changes are accurate. Such techniques could be helpful for all L2 writing audiences, but for different reasons. "Eye" learners tend to play it safe, using only vocabulary and grammar structures they are comfortable with, so encouraging and training them to vary their approach could broaden their knowledge of English academic writing. "Ear" learners, as noted elsewhere, may have a larger everyday vocabulary and are more comfortable with a variety of sentence structures, but they may need to be trained to substitute more academic vocabulary and syntax for the informal, conversational language in their texts.[4]

To summarize this discussion, the intentional, explicit development of academic language—vocabulary and grammar—is a subject that in recent years has received much attention from researchers but has been less likely to be adopted by teachers. There are several reasons for this. For one, many teachers do not have the linguistic background themselves to analyze vocabulary and grammar choices, let alone present lessons, analysis tasks, and strategy training around those structures (see Conrad, 2008). In addition, teachers working with students at lower levels of L2 proficiency are (appropriately) more focused on helping students cross the linguistic threshold that will help them to read and write simple L2 texts. Emphasizing style, variety, and sophistication does not seem to many teachers an important pedagogical objective at this stage of L2 development. Finally, even when teachers feel competent to present such information and are teaching more advanced L2 students, they may not grasp how to incorporate this kind of academic language development into a busy reading/writing/language class syllabus. However, in college-level settings and especially when the audience includes students who are well beyond beginner or novice levels in L2 acquisition (i.e., early-arriving residents and very advanced international student), teachers must move their focus beyond the basic threshold levels and toward an informed, real-world approach to developing students' academic language and literacy skills (see Reid, 2008, for a collection that develops this theme in a variety of very practical ways).

Developing Reading and Writing Strategies and Processes

Because L2 students from different backgrounds may have diverse experiences with reading and writing in the L2, it can be important for teachers, informed by detailed knowledge of their students' educational backgrounds (see Chapters 3–4), to design reading strategy instruction and writing process instruction based on students' points of greatest need.

As to reading instruction (see Chapter 4), students educated in their home countries may have limited experience with reading extensively and reading fluently (or quickly). They may have well-honed skills in the intensive, close analysis of short academic or literary texts, but they may be overwhelmed if asked to read more than a page or two in an ESL class and quite intimidated by the substantial reading requirements in content courses across the disciplines. Further, due to cross-linguistic differences as well as prior experiences, they may read too slowly for adequate comprehension (Birch, 2007). Such students can benefit from extensive reading assignments and opportunities, which may include teacher-selected readings of adequate length and difficulty (see, among others, Seymour & Walsh, 2006) as well as self-selected reading of newspapers, magazines, and books of various genres. The benefits of extensive reading for L2 learners are well established in the literature (Day & Bamford, 1998; Hedgcock & Ferris, 2009; Krashen, 2004; Seymour & Walsh, 2006; Spack, 1997/2004), and there is a variety of practical suggestions available for teachers who want to implement extensive reading programs:

- Apprise students about the ways in which extensive reading can help them to succeed academically. This is especially important for students whose prior L2 reading experience is limited to close, classroom-based intensive analysis of texts; they may not immediately see the connection between, for example, reading *Newsweek* or a novel and succeeding in their college coursework.

- Help students find interesting reading materials that are appropriate to their language and reading levels.

- Provide classroom support in the form of time for sustained silent reading, book discussion groups, and oral reports that allow students to read and to share with others about what they are reading.

- Establish some kind of structure and accountability (a percentage of the course grade or extra credit; reading logs, oral/written reports or summaries, recommendations, posters) so that students actually do the reading regularly and do not procrastinate. However, it is important that such accountability mechanisms not be too onerous or difficult so that students find extensive reading enjoyable and not simply another chore or homework assignment.

Teachers can also address the fluency and reading speed issue by implementing timed reading, reading rate, or fluency-building activities as a small but regular part of the reading lesson (e.g., ten minutes per day, three days per week). Suggestions and resources for fluency-building are plentiful (see, e.g., Birch, 2007; Jensen, 1986) and include these general suggestions:

- Choose texts that are short (400–800 words), comprehensible, and accessible.
- Decide on a timing system and explain it clearly to the students.
- Show the students how to maintain reading rate charts (words per minute; accuracy).
- Use timed reading consistently (every day or several times per week).
- Encourage students to measure their own progress, not compete against class-mates (Hedgcock & Ferris, 2009).

While L2 students who are newcomers to the United States may especially benefit from or need an emphasis on building fluency (through the seemingly opposite techniques of reading rate and extensive reading activities), students who have spent years in U.S. educational settings may already have experience with extensive reading in English and little need for timed reading exercises. However, they may especially benefit from explicit instruction and practice in intensive reading strategies (Aebersold & Field, 1997; Hedgcock & Ferris, 2009; Grabe & Stoller, 2002; Hudson, 2007; Seymour & Walsh, 2006) for academic texts, for instance:

- previewing a text to get a sense of its general content, important sub-topics, organizational structure, and significant language (e.g., key terms that are important and used frequently)
- rereading a text several times to analyze and review different aspects of it
- using highlighting and annotating techniques to actively interact with the text and to provide information for effectively reviewing the text
- creating and using graphic organizers to identify and organize important information
- applying a variety of strategies to cope with unfamiliar vocabulary (e.g., using surrounding context to guess at meaning; skipping items that seem less important; analyzing word parts; using the dictionary)
- summarizing, questioning, and responding to a text as a means to check comprehension, make inferences, and think critically about the ideas

Many students have never learned these strategies, nor have they had much experience with the types of intensive reading of academic texts expected in post-secondary contexts. Most secondary English instruction focuses on literary texts; to the extent there is close analysis, it tends to focus on literary features (plot, conflict, theme, imagery, rhyme/meter, etc.).[5] As a result, even monolingual native English speakers arriving in college may struggle with the types of reading assignments required across the disciplines. Late- and early-arriving resident L2 students may have spent some of their secondary years in sheltered English or ESL courses that provided even less preparation for post-secondary academic work. Further, their overall exposure to the language is still not equivalent to that of their monolingual peers (see Chapter 2).

It is important to qualify this discussion by observing that newcomer "eye" learner students can certainly benefit from intensive reading lessons and that U.S.-educated students could also profit from extensive reading. For that matter, most monolingual native English speakers beginning college today could also benefit from both emphases. For the classroom teacher, the differences lie in *balance and degree of emphasis* of these different approaches. Further, the teacher needs to be informed by understanding students' characteristics and backgrounds so that texts selected and other instructional choices provide optimal experiences for a specific group of students (see Chapter 4).

With regard to writing strategies and processes, composition is not universally taught in other educational systems—either in L1 or L2—and the United States emphasis on process-oriented, multiple-draft composing may also be new to some students. Most U.S.-educated students, from elementary school on, will have had some experience with writing workshop activities such as freewriting, clustering, outlining, drafting, revising, collaborating, and sharing finished products with others. They also have typically been taught and required to produce the five-paragraph essay and are used to being evaluated with analytic grading rubrics. Some or all of these techniques may be unfamiliar to newcomers educated elsewhere. Further, the prior writing instruction received by some U.S.-educated L2 students may also have been inadequate or ineffective for a variety of reasons.

College instructors of L2 writers may therefore need to teach (or reinforce) helpful writing strategies or processes, not only for success in the composition course but also for writing in other college/university classes. The teacher might consider some or all of these instructional goals for writing:

- helping students understand assignment specifications and audience needs
- helping students to generate or gather ideas for writing
- helping students know how to present or organize their content for a variety of genres or assignments
- helping students incorporate ideas from other authors/texts/sources into their own writing
- helping students learn how to give and receive feedback to and from peers and how to consider and utilize feedback from others (peers, teachers, tutors)

- helping students manage their time throughout the writing process by adding intermediate deadlines so that they have adequate opportunities to think about, revise, and edit their work

- helping students look critically (for revision) and carefully (for editing) at their own texts

In addition, teachers whose classes include international students or late-arriving residents might also consider presenting insights from contrastive or intercultural rhetoric research (Connor, 1996, 2003; Ferris & Hedgcock, 2005; Kaplan, 1966; Leki, 1992; Reid, 2006a) that might help students understand the conventions and expectations of the U.S. academic discourse community(ies) with regard to types of evidence used, organizational patterns, appropriate amounts of elaboration, and attribution of sources (and avoidance of plagiarism). This information would be less relevant or unnecessary for learners who are not literate in their L1 (i.e., many early-arriving residents).

As already noted, teachers of L2 students of any description and even those with mixed classes of monolingual and multilingual students could profitably consider and include any or all of these approaches or suggestions to building academic reading and writing strategies and processes. However, an understanding of the different audiences' backgrounds and the specific needs they bring to the classroom will help teachers sort through various priorities and design courses and lessons that will best meet the needs of a particular group of learners.

Feedback

Providing or facilitating feedback to learners is another critical sub-topic in surveying the instructional implications of diverse L2 student audiences in college. In academic settings, feedback is provided in a number of ways and for a variety of purposes:

- **Informal feedback** during class lessons or discussions helps students to know on the spot whether they have, for instance, defined a target lexical item accurately, comprehended a text fully, or identified a grammatical structure correctly.

- **Assessment,** in this context specifically meaning graded/corrected assignments or tests, provides learners with information—the grade/score itself and any verbal corrections or comments—about the progress they are making in learning course content and/or mastering the language/literacy skills being covered in the syllabus.

- **Commentary** on preliminary drafts of assignments—papers or projects—is intended to help students rethink or improve their work before it is finalized.

- **Language-focused feedback** is designed to help students correct/edit errors they have made in their written texts and/or analyze their word- and sentence-level choices to consider possible alternatives.

Most published discussions of teacher (and/or peer) feedback focus primarily or exclusively on the final two types of feedback, but it is important to understand that all the purposes of feedback typically operate simultaneously in a college-level language or reading/writing course and that the diverse student audiences we have discussed in this book will—or should—influence the feedback approaches that teachers may take. The differences may affect students' understanding of the *teacher's purposes in feedback* and of the *content and form* of feedback as well as their reactions to the *methods* for delivery of feedback.

Feedback Purposes

U.S.-trained instructors (especially those trained in composition) may have a clear understanding of why and how they should provide feedback to student writers. As to the *why,* they understand that their feedback is intended to help students revise current texts and/or utilize lessons learned in subsequent written assignments, not merely to impose their will, to tell students what they did wrong, or to justify a grade. As to the *how,* they have likely been warned against methods of giving feedback that appropriates or takes over a student's text, leading to advice such as "use questions, not statements or imperatives," and "respond as an interested reader, not an evaluator or judge." Particularly with regard to this latter point, they may feel a strong degree of discomfort with responding at all, fearing that they will discourage, demoralize, or demotivate students.

However, students raised and educated in other cultures (i.e., newcomers such as international students or late-arriving residents) may have a much more hierarchical view of teacher-student relationships and have little awareness of, let alone understanding of or concern about, U.S. teachers' anxieties about power dynamics and differentials. In short, they are likely to regard any information from the teacher as something they must obey without question and would be confused or even amused by U.S. teachers' concerns about student "ownership" of a paper or appropriation issues (see Ferris, 2003, and Reid, 1994, for additional discussion of response/appropriation with regard to L2 writers). Further, if students have not encountered writing process approaches to instruction—multiple drafting, collaboration, portfolios, response-and-revision cycles—they may not understand that the teacher is trying to guide them through a series of iterations or steps as a paper or project evolves. Thus, they may neither revise/edit effectively nor understand how to use feedback in revision/editing (or even that they *should* use it). Because of this potential mismatch between teacher expectations and student experience, it is important for the teacher to explain and reiterate the processes and procedures used in the class, including the role of feedback in the process.

Content and Form of Feedback

Composition scholars have posed the question of whether indirect methods of teacher feedback are optimal for student writers, particularly L2 writers (e.g.,

Conrad & Goldstein, 1999; Ferris, 1997, 2001; Ferris, Pezone, Tade, & Tinti, 1997; Goldstein, 2005; Goldstein & Conrad, 1990; Newkirk, 1995; Patthey-Chavez & Ferris, 1997; Reid, 1994). As already noted, U.S.-trained writing teachers are often urged to avoid "teacherly" responses in favor of "readerly" ones, including using questions rather than imperatives and engaging in a "dialogue in the margins" rather than simply evaluating or judging text quality. However, cultural differences with regard to teacher-student power dynamics as well as limited experience with writing process techniques (response, revision, portfolios) may result in confusion on the part of students about teacher intent and meaning if comments or suggestions are too veiled in an effort to appear less hierarchical.

With regard to questions in particular, text analytic research on teacher commentary has identified at least three distinct question types (see Ferris, 1997, 2001):

- **Type 1**: Request for information known to the writer: *What is your major?*

- **Type 2:** Indirect request phrased as a yes-no question: *Can you give an example here?*

- **Type 3:** "Higher-order" question to challenge writer's thinking, logic, or argument: *Isn't it true that . . . ? Have you considered . . . ?*

Research on the effects of teacher questions on L2 student revisions has suggested that Type 1 questions are utilized the most successfully and that Type 3 questions are the most problematic, often being ignored by student writers or leading to ineffective changes or even deletions of the "offending" text portion (Conrad & Goldstein, 1999; Ferris, 1997, 2001). The problem with Type 3 questions in particular is that they not only are more abstract and cognitively difficult but they also may well necessitate a fairly major reworking of the existing text rather than micro-level changes (suggested by Type 1 questions and to a lesser degree by Type 2 questions) requiring the addition or change of perhaps only a few words or a sentence or two. With regard to Type 2 questions, which in pragmatic terms constitute an indirect speech act, it has also been noted that newcomer students unfamiliar with pragmatic moves in English may actually interpret them as literal yes-no questions ("Well, yes, I *could* provide an example, but I don't really *want* to") (Ferris, 1995, 1997, 1999, 2001, 2003).

These insights have implications for teacher responding strategies. First, teachers should endeavor to make their feedback clear, text-specific, and helpful. Suggestions that are misunderstood by L2 student writers will not help them to improve the text at hand or to develop as writers. Second, teachers should be particularly careful in using questions—not avoiding them necessarily but certainly assessing whether the question is straightforward enough to assist student writers in revision. Third, teachers should give students opportunities to ask questions about feedback they have received and should discuss and practice revision strategies in class so that students understand the value and utility of feedback they have received.

Another issue with regard to the form and content of teacher feedback pertains to the specific instance of error correction. As I and others have written elsewhere, written corrective feedback (WCF) has the potential to aid students' short- and long-term writing development if it is approached thoughtfully and carefully (Bitchener, 2008; Bitchener, Young, & Cameron, 2005; Ellis, Sheen, Murakami, & Takashima, 2008; Ferris, 2002, 2003, 2004; Ferris & Hedgcock, 2005; Sheen, 2007). However, it is critically important that teachers consider students' differing knowledge bases in providing language-focused feedback. For example, "eye" learners who learned English in classrooms in their home countries may have a much firmer grasp on grammar rules and accompanying metalinguistic terminology than do "ear" learners who acquired English in naturalistic settings rather than formally (Ferris, 1999, 2006; Ferris & Roberts, 2001; Reid, 1998/2006b, 2006a; see Chapter 2). Teachers should thus be careful about utilizing such metalanguage or related correction codes (e.g., *vt* for "verb tense") in their written feedback, only using it when they are certain that such feedback will indeed elicit prior student knowledge. As for "ear" learners, particularly early-arriving residents, research suggests that they may be able to utilize their acquired intuitions about correctness to edit errors once they have been pointed out through less explicit methods (e.g., underlining or highlighting errors but without reference to grammar terms or correction codes) (Ferris, 2006; Ferris & Roberts, 2001; Robb, Ross, & Shortreed, 1986)—but such methods might not provide enough information to "eye" learners.

Feedback Delivery Methods

A final practical issue to consider with regard to feedback is *how* feedback should be given—through written comments/corrections, through face-to-face interactions—and by whom. While many L1 and L2 teachers are passionate advocates of one-to-one teacher-student conferences as the best means to deliver feedback about both content and language, extensive conferencing is not always practical in large classes or in settings (such as community colleges) where teachers may be part-time or adjunct and may not be able to hold office hours (or even have offices). With regard to varying student L2 audiences, conferences may also be stressful especially to newcomers (recently arrived international and late-arriving resident students), who may be uncomfortable with such interactions for cultural reasons and, more significantly, because they tax their more limited oral/aural resources. In short, these students may benefit more from written commentary because it can be processed visually and reviewed, rather than having to remember what was discussed in a conference (which they may not have understood fully). Teachers who wish to keep the option of conferencing open with newcomers may need to provide additional support in the form of explaining or structuring expectations for the conference, encouraging the student to take written notes and/or to audiotape the conference, or even providing some kind of written record themselves of suggestions for students to take with them (see Arndt, 1993).

As to the *who* of feedback, much has been written about the benefits and drawbacks of utilizing peer feedback with L2 writers (see, e.g., Jacobs, Curtis, Braine, & Huang, 1998; Ferris, 2003; Ferris & Hedgcock, 2005; Liu & Hansen, 2002; Reid, 2006a; Zhang, 1995, 1999). While peer feedback is a valuable pedagogical technique for a variety of well-documented reasons, it must be handled carefully by the teacher, particularly when working with diverse L2 student audiences. Early-arriving students who are accustomed to U.S. classrooms will likely have had extensive experience with group work and collaboration, including peer feedback on writing. International and late-arriving resident students, on the other hand, may be confused by the practice ("Why am I receiving feedback from other language learners rather than the teacher?") and even embarrassed or threatened by it, fearing a loss of face. Teachers can address these issues and reap the considerable benefits of peer response by considering the following steps in implementing peer feedback:

- discussing the benefits of peer response and possible problems with the class

- modeling peer response by having the class discuss a sample student paper, using the same peer response task specifications they will apply with each other's papers

- structuring peer response and peer editing tasks carefully so that students know what to do and what not to do (e.g., "underline in pencil any problems with verb tense that you see, but do not make any corrections")

- creating peer response pairs and groups carefully rather than randomly

- utilizing peer response consistently so that students become more comfortable with it and improve their responding skills

- validating peer response activities by requiring students to reflect upon their peers' suggestions and discuss what changes they might (or might not) make as a result

- holding students accountable for peer response by collecting and grading written peer response forms and by making part of the paper/course grade contingent on thoughtful engagement with the process (including cooperation, collaboration, revision, and editing)

- regularly soliciting student input and feedback about classroom peer response activities to pinpoint any problems and make adjustments as necessary

Finally, of course, it is important to note that teachers (intentionally or not) model effective or ineffective responding to students through their own responding behaviors, whether through written or oral feedback. If a teacher is vague, unclear, discouraging, or excessively focused on form, it is likely that peer respondents will follow that example as well (see Connor & Asenavage, 1994).

Feedback of all types is critically important to the success of any learning situation. Middle school math students need clear feedback about their approach to math concepts and problems, and L2 college students need feedback about both their use of language and their strategies for dealing with language and reading/writing tasks. This discussion is closed by simply reiterating that teachers must be thoughtful and intentional about the principles and strategies that guide their classroom feedback and assessment, and that considerations of varying student audiences can and should inform such decision-making.

Additional Support

An important topic to consider in this chapter on classroom instruction is what happens *outside* of the classroom to support and promote L2 students' language/literacy development. In addition to issues already discussed such as teacher-student interaction and feedback, it is also useful to understand and examine additional support services that may be available to students in various contexts. Many or most colleges and universities have some variation or combination of learning centers, writing centers, or language/reading/writing labs. Many offer peer tutoring (from trained students) or more expert tutoring or small-group adjunct tutorials or workshops conducted by faculty or staff (e.g., paid lab tutors). In addition, students may have campus- or community-based opportunities to obtain private tutoring. Another avenue for out-of-class support is additional materials or resources that the teacher can recommend—textbooks, handbooks, software programs, or websites.

For several reasons, it is important that teachers be aware of such resources and thoughtful about helping students to utilize them. First, it can be difficult or impossible for busy teachers to meet all the needs of each individual student in their classes. As argued throughout this book, it is a daunting challenge for L2 students to pursue educational goals in post-secondary settings, and they need a variety of support systems to be successful. L2 college students are at risk of giving up and dropping out at a number of points in their education: when they first matriculate and many must complete remedial language/writing instruction; when they move into general education and then upper-division or graduate-level major coursework, in which language and literacy demands become increasingly more difficult; and when they must meet upper-division writing proficiency or writing-intensive requirements in order to graduate. In short, L2 college/university students need a great deal of support, and even the most competent and caring L2 teacher cannot provide everything they will need.

Second, in many U.S. college settings, the L2 student audience is very diverse, and in-class instruction may meet the needs of some students but not others. For example, in a given college language, reading, or composition course, smaller groups of students may need specialized instruction on strategies for intensive academic reading, vocabulary development, paragraph and essay structure, the writing process, and specific points of grammar (which may vary within the class based on L1 backgrounds as well as prior instruction—or lack thereof). It is not practical or appropriate for a teacher to provide whole-class lessons on issues that only a subset of the students actually need, so it may become necessary to direct students to various out-of-class resources.

However, as any experienced teacher knows, the mere *existence* of such resources does not ensure their *quality,* their *accessibility*, or their *appropriateness* for all (or any) L2 students. For example, as discussed in Chapter 3, it is well known that campus writing centers in many contexts cannot or will not provide the kind of specialized support that L2 writers need (see Bruce & Rafoth, 2004). Thus, it is not adequate for a teacher merely to tell students to "get tutoring" or "go to the lab" or to provide a handout with a list of campus labs and tutoring centers. Nor is it useful for a teacher to vaguely suggest that students consult handbooks or websites if they need further information. Rather, teachers must research these options in their particular context and with their mix of students in mind and make informed, precise recommendations. It may also be necessary for L2 teachers in college/university settings to become advocates and resource persons for the further *development and improvement* of campus support systems.

Considerations for "Mixed" (Mainstream and Multilingual) Classes

Suggestions made or issues raised in discussing any or all of the sub-topics apply equally or even to a greater degree in mainstream composition courses in which monolingual and multilingual students are studying side by side. Previous considerations with regard to classroom interaction, feedback, language development, and outside support are extremely important in such settings. Further, instructors in such settings need to be especially careful to investigate and assess students' backgrounds and language/academic literacy development (see Chapters 3–4) so that they can provide extra attention and assistance to L2 students in their classes.

It may be helpful at this point in the discussion to introduce the ad hoc construct of what I have come to call "the invisible and underserved middle" of the L2 student population. When one considers the multilingual/ESL/L2 population at a college or university, in many cases there is a top, a bottom, and a middle layer of student knowledge and proficiency. L2 writing instructors tend to focus on the bottom, the true English learners (or "incipient bilinguals") who obviously need ESL instruction and support to succeed in English-medium college studies. Composition instructors may instead focus on the top, the well assimilated early-arriving L2 student whose differences from other students are barely noticeable and not that problematic, or the highly educated international student whose knowledge of English grammar is better than their own. Probably both groups of professionals would agree that the bottom layer of students needs ESL classes and the top layer will succeed in mainstream classes.

In between, though, is the "invisible middle." These students may be orally fluent and able to compose academic essays of adequate length, but they may have a variety of language and literacy issues (see Chapter 2) that hold them back from being truly successful. They have gaps and they have problems, but their issues are not as apparent and pressing as those of the bottom layer of students, nor are they able to be as self-sufficient and successful as those in the top layer. This "invisible middle" layer of students may end up divided between ESL classes and mainstream writing classes. It is those students who need extra attention and whose instructors really need to be prepared to help them. But they are often underserved for several interacting reasons:

1. Because they appear fluent, assimilated, and comfortable in the classroom (or do not call much attention to themselves) and because their writing issues are visible but not egregious, teachers overlook or underestimate their specialized needs.

2. Because composition instructors often value and privilege "writing processes" and "thinking skills" and place less priority on language, they do not prioritize assisting students with language issues, either in their classroom instruction or in individual feedback.

3. Because many writing instructors are not well trained in grammar or language development, even if they recognize the language gaps and feel that it is important to address them, they may not feel equipped or qualified to do so.

These three factors are complex, involving specific classroom issues (1), differing cultures and values among composition programs and professionals (2), and teacher preparation (3) (also discussed in Chapters 3 and 6 of this volume; see also Ferris, 2002, Chapter 3). Teachers in "mixed" composition courses must research and assess their students' backgrounds and abilities, and they must take seriously the academic literacy needs especially of their L2 students and take steps in and out of class to address them. Multilingual students are no longer simply the responsibility (or the "problem") of the ESL program; *all* instructors, programs, and institutions must seriously consider what these students need to be successful and develop materials, techniques, and support services to help them be successful.

Chapter 5 tackled the extremely large topic of adapting classroom instruction in recognition of the characteristics and needs of an increasingly diverse L2 student audience. With no attempt to be comprehensive in coverage, several sub-topics for consideration and discussion were identified: classroom interaction, academic language and literacy development, feedback, and support systems outside of the classroom. All of these issues and suggestions are equally relevant, if not more so, in "mixed" settings in which monolingual native speakers and L2 students are taught together. Readers can and should investigate these various sub-topics more thoroughly.

QUESTIONS FOR REFLECTION AND DISCUSSION

1. The first section of this chapter discussed several classroom interaction issues and possible solutions to potential problems. From your own experience and observation, can you add any other possible problems, and what ideas do you have for solving them? If possible, interview a language, writing, or disciplinary faculty member whose classes include L2 students, asking him/her about the various issues raised in this section. Does that instructor confirm, contradict, or have anything to add to this sub-topic?

2. The section on academic language development gave a number of specific ideas about how to help students build a more effective vocabulary for reading and writing. Were any of these ideas new to you? Do you have any concerns or problems with any of them?

3. The section on teaching intensive reading strategies and writing processes provided lists of specific skills to consider. If possible, look at one or more L2 reading, writing, or reading/writing textbooks and see if you can identify exercises or activities designed to help students develop these strategies and processes. Also consider ways you might use or adapt the materials depending on the "mix" of L2 students in a particular class.

4. The section on feedback presented several principles for providing clear and effective feedback to L2 writers. Think of your own experiences in receiving feedback from teachers or professors and/or any experience you have had in giving feedback to students as a teacher or tutor. What are some of your observations, concerns, or struggles regarding providing feedback to L2 writers? Do any of the ideas in this section provide some clarity or food for further thought?

5. The final section introduced the idea of the "invisible middle" of the L2 student audience in U.S. colleges/universities. Have you encountered—as a student or as a teacher—L2 students who are quietly struggling in mainstream college courses? What do you think L2 specialists and mainstream instructors can or should do to be more aware of and better serve such students?

CHAPTER ENDNOTES

[1] For teacher-friendly in-depth treatments, readers might consider the following texts, depending upon time, interest, and availability of material:

Teaching L2 reading: Aebersold & Field (1997); Birch (2007); Grabe & Stoller (2002); Hedgcock & Ferris (2009); Hudson (2007); Seymour & Walsh (2006).

Teaching L2 writing: Blanton & Kroll (2002); Casanave (2004); Ferris & Hedgcock (2005); Hyland (2002); Kroll (2003); Matsuda, Cox, Jordan, & Ortmeier-Hooper (2006b); Reid (1998/2006b; 2008); Scarcella (2003).

Reading/writing connections: Hirvela (2004)

Teaching L2 vocabulary: Coxhead (2006); Coxhead & Byrd (2007); Folse (2004)

Teaching L2 academic listening/speaking skills: Flowerdew (1994); Murphy (2006).

Response to L2 student writing: Bates, Lane, & Lange (1993); Ferris (2002, 2003); Goldstein (2005); Hyland & Hyland (2006); Liu & Hansen (2002).

[2] The studies by Ferris & Tagg (1996a, 1996b) and Ferris (1998) asked survey respondents (both professors and students) about the "status" of the students (international or immigrant) but did not distinguish between late-arriving and early-arriving residents. That information was used for descriptive purposes but not for statistical cross-tabulation with survey responses.

[3] For research on L2 vocabulary acquisition, see Folse (2004); Nation (2001); Schmitt & McCarthy (1997); Schmitt (2000). For syntax, see Schleppegrell (2004); Schleppegrell & Colombi (2002). For focus-on-form and research on corrective feedback in SLA, see Bitchener (2008); Bitchener & Knoch (2008); Doughty & Williams (1998); Ellis (2004); Ellis, Loewen, & Erlam (2006); Sheen (2007).

[4] In an articulate and thought-provoking recent paper on the role of vocabulary instruction in writing classes, Folse (2008) notes that it is unfair to ask students to "use their own words" in discussing textual sources and accuse them of "plagiarism" when their own active vocabulary is not developed enough to permit competent paraphrasing.

[5] Though standards-based secondary education is changing the focus on literary analysis somewhat, in actual practice these changes are slow in coming and in some contexts non-existent.

PART 3
Applications

Chapter 6

Serving Diverse L2 Student Audiences: Where Do We Go from Here?

> . . . an institution has a moral and ethical responsibility to provide English language courses and/ or other language assistance to the nonnative English speaking (NNES) students it accepts into its various degree programs.
>
> —Kroll, 2006, p. 297

Tʜɪs ʙᴏᴏᴋ ʜᴀs ᴇxᴀᴍɪɴᴇᴅ ᴛʜᴇ ᴄʜᴀɴɢɪɴɢ ɴᴀᴛᴜʀᴇ of the L2 student audience in U.S. colleges and universities and discussed the implications of understanding these audiences for program design, course planning, and classroom instruction. Chapter 6 summarizes the various threads of discussion (which thus far have implicitly addressed the question of *Where are we now?*) and makes suggestions regarding possible programmatic and instructional models as well as an agenda for future research investigations. Specifically, these questions are addressed:

- What are some promising models and approaches currently being utilized?
- Considering the student audience issues raised in this book, what are general principles for (more) effective program/course/lesson design going forward?
- What important questions should future research projects investigate?

Students' Own Voices

First, we revisit the three audience prototypes—John, Hector, and Luciana— introduced in Chapters 1–2. What might they say about their experiences in American universities, and how might others like them be better served in the future?

John, the international student struggling to finish his undergraduate degree, might say something like this:

> If an American university is going to recruit and admit international students, it has an obligation to provide the right types of support for them as they move through the degree program.

> A campus international student office is a good start, but it is not enough. Why is it that I have passed my major courses and nearly completed my degree but I still cannot write well enough in English to meet graduation requirements? English majors and graduate student tutors in the campus writing center are helpful, but they need specialized knowledge about how to work with L2 writers. In short—you brought me here, you took my money (a great deal more than a resident student would pay), and I put in a lot of time and effort pursuing my degree. You owe me the kinds of assessments, structures and support I need to be successful.

Hector, the 19-year-old late-arriving resident student from Mexico who was immediately mainstreamed into a first-year composition course at his university, might add this:

> I appreciate the opportunity to live and study in the U.S. However, I am a bit worried. *Huckleberry Finn* was hard for me to read—I think I got the main points in the plot (a Spanish-language *SparkNotes* commentary helped a lot[1])—but there were many words and details I didn't understand at all, though I managed to hide this from my teacher and classmates. I also know that my writing has a lot of mistakes and that it does not look much like the writing of my peers in the class. But my teacher does not help me much with this—she has written notes like "watch your grammar" or "consider seeing a tutor" on my paper, but she never teaches any grammar in class and she has never talked to me outside of class. Even though I may seem to be "doing OK" in the class, I worry that my English reading and writing will not be good enough for my future studies. I wish my English teacher knew more about how to discern my needs and to help me, and I wish that I had the choice to take an ESL writing class instead, or maybe even a reading or grammar tutorial outside of class. Even an ESL writing tutor to meet with every week would probably help a lot.

Luciana, the early-arriving resident student in a mainstream basic writing course, might say this:

> I am glad to be in a regular English class. I was born in California and am a U.S. citizen who graduated from a U.S. high school, so I am not an "ESL" student like those students who just came here recently to study. But I am still very worried about succeeding in college. The university says that if I do

not pass my basic writing course in one year, I will be disen-
rolled, so I feel a lot of pressure. My teacher is very nice
and supportive, but she is a graduate student herself, and
she has never had training in working with second language
students. I think I have good ideas, but I don't always have
the grammar or the vocabulary to put them together in a paper
correctly. My English teacher gives us interesting articles
to read and discuss, but they are pretty long—sometimes 8
or 10 pages—and I have never enjoyed reading very much;
the readings also have a lot of long sentences and difficult
vocabulary. My teacher says I shouldn't worry so much about
language because my ideas and my writing process are more
important, anyway. I still worry about my writing, though—I
know I make a lot of mistakes, and I don't really feel like I
am getting any better. I wish my teacher or the Writing Center would figure out ways to help me improve my writing and
my reading. I still wouldn't want to be in an ESL class, but I
wish the English teaching and tutoring would better fit what
I need. I really wonder if I will make it through college—or
even make it through this class.

These hypothetical student commentaries accurately capture the struggles of
the three different student prototypes and the ways in which their institutions could
provide better support for them. The truth is that real students most likely do not, in
the moment, understand the degree to which their current program is failing them.
It is only later, when they struggle to meet the demands of general education and
major courses—when they perhaps fail an upper-division writing assessment or
when they cannot enter the kind of job or advanced degree program they desire—
that they may realize how underprepared they actually are. Even then they might
not understand the internal workings of university and program bureaucracy well
enough to accurately assess what *could have and should have* been done to help
them throughout their college/university studies. Many, facing financial pressures
and the stresses of keeping up with difficult coursework—which only increase
as they go into the upper levels of post-secondary instruction—simply drop out,
discouraged, frustrated, and demoralized. This sad outcome may not be inevitable
for John, Hector, and Luciana, but as things stand, it will be for many of their peers.
What can we learn and do to improve the odds for their success?

Current Models

To prepare to write this book and this chapter, I conducted an informal survey
of what colleges and universities around the United States are presently doing
to most effectively identify, assess, and serve the various audiences of L2 students

at their institutions. Utilizing contacts made through the TESOL Second Language Writing Interest Section listserv, I distributed informal surveys (see Appendix) that were completed and returned to me via email, in some cases with additional materials (course descriptions, syllabi, etc.) attached.[2] In addition, I spoke to several coordinators/instructors in programs in California that I knew to be on the cutting edge of these student audience issues.[3] Several productive themes emerged in these informal discussions or email responses:

- creation of new course options to serve an increasingly diverse population

- development of various types of support services, especially for L2 students in mainstream composition courses

- collaboration among ESL/English/Composition faculty to best place and serve multilingual students

Each is briefly discussed. It must be emphasized, however, that these successful and forward-looking models are highlighted not because they are common or frequently found but rather because they are still relatively rare. Still, outlining them might provide administrators and instructors with some ideas that could be adapted to their own contexts.

Innovative Course Options

Chapter 3 noted that in various programs around the United States, there are separate course placement options for L2 students at the remedial and/or college level (i.e., separate but equivalent ESL courses). Several programs have taken these special-ized course options a step further. For example, one California State University campus[4] has designed distinct sections of upper-division writing courses for resident and international ESL populations (in addition to a "mainstream" option). What is different among these courses is the texts/topics and student goals/needs on which they focus. For instance, in the course for residents, reading/writing assignments may draw on the students' immigrant or multilingual/multicultural experiences, and course goals are designed with the understanding that the students will be living and working in the United States. In contrast, the international student–focused ESL course draws on students' experiences in their home countries and is structured with the understanding that students will be returning home after completing their studies in the United States. Students may enroll in any of the three courses (which all have different course numbers) to fulfill the requirements but are advised by their instructors about the distinctions so that they can make the choice that best meets their needs and interests.

Another innovative model is "designated sections" of college-level writing courses—with the designation meaning that instructors with specialized training in working with L2 writers will be teaching those sections. To put it another way, it is the *teachers* who are designated for specific sections, not the students. Again, students may enroll in whichever sections they prefer, but they will be told by the program/instructor about the differences among sections so that they can make an informed decision.

Finally, Christine Holten (2002), in the special Generation 1.5 theme issue of the *CATESOL Journal,* describes a writing course (English 2I) at UCLA that was specially designed for early-arriving resident students; the course provides additional class hours (six instead of the four in the corresponding English 2 or ESL 35 courses), a slower pace (fewer reading/writing assignments that can be explored in greater depth), and increased attention to grammar and vocabulary. This course is still operating at UCLA today, and Holten describes it as unique because it represents an effective cross-departmental collaboration between the ESL and English composition program. Two important characteristics of all three models are: (1) Students can choose which course option best suits them, and they are not forced into or out of mainstream or ESL courses; and (2) The course titles do not make any reference to ESL or multilingual students (though such terms may be found in the catalog course descriptions).[5] This latter point is important because many L2 students arriving at four-year universities are concerned about the possible stigma of having an ESL class on their transcripts, worrying that future graduate programs or employers might not consider those courses equivalent or rigorous enough.

My survey of existing course offerings was not intended to be comprehensive but rather to identify possible models that other institutions might consider. There are likely variations on the courses described around the United States, but they do not appear to be widespread at this point in time.

Support Services

Many of the respondents to my email survey described various types of support provided for L2 students on their campuses. For instance, at one small liberal arts college, the respondent, the sole L2 writing specialist on the campus, spends most of her time meeting individually with L2 students (mostly U.S. residents) or talking with subject-matter instructors about the progress of these students in their classes and ways in which she and the professor could both provide specialized support. As the college is very small, there are relatively few L2 students, so she feels that the individualized system is effective in meeting students' needs (though she did wish that there were a few more L2 specialists available). This particular model is not especially transferable to larger schools with many more L2 students, but the principle—that a trained L2 specialist can be an advocate for students and provide individual advice to faculty as well as L2 students themselves—is one worth exploring and adopting on a larger scale.

In several other programs, L2 students in either ESL or mainstream writing courses are matched up from the beginning of the term with one-to-one tutoring services (usually with a trained peer tutor). The idea is that rather than simply telling students to "go to the Writing Center" or "find a tutor" (and hoping that they follow through and that the tutors they find are capable of helping them), tutors will be trained and assigned directly to those students identified as needing additional support as they complete their writing requirements. The principle behind this model is a frank recognition that it is especially challenging for L2 students to succeed in university courses, and that even with well trained teachers and specialized course options, most or all of them need or could benefit from regular, individualized assistance from a consistent and competent source (a tutor assigned directly to them).

Administrators and instructors at large schools with increasing numbers of L2 students might counter that, while dedicated one-to-one assistance for L2 students might be ideal, it is not practical given limited financial and human resources. Adaptations of the model might include having tutors and staff with L2 training always available at campus writing or learning centers (see Destandau & Wald, 2002; Wolfe-Quintero & Segade, 1999) so that students seeking those resources would not encounter the roadblocks faced by our early-arriving prototype, Luciana, and her peers. Another model might include small-group assistance in the form of workshops taught by the writing program or writing center, adjunct tutorials (adjunct either to specific writing courses and/or specific subject-matter courses). Small-group models, while not one-to-one, at least provide students with extra instruction and attention beyond what they might receive in a larger composition course. In any case, it seems clear that access to various types of support services is critical for L2 students throughout their post-secondary careers, and that colleges and universities need to think creatively and productively about ways to provide those services, to connect students to them, and to make them operate most effectively.

Faculty Collaboration

In the cutting-edge course options described and those from my email survey responses, the presence or absence of collaboration among faculty—in writing programs and across the disciplines—emerged as an important theme. Holten (2002) notes that a key to the successful development of the English 21 course for Generation 1.5 writers at UCLA was the cooperation of English and ESL faculty (who are in two distinct programs) to identify the student audience, design the course, and create institutional pathways for the most appropriate students to enroll in it. Also, because of the difficulty in many settings of correctly identifying L2 students (see Chapter 3), communication and collaboration among administrators and instructors making placement decisions is critical.

Finally, a number of the survey respondents described scenarios in which L2 students were mainstreamed into first-year composition courses after doing remedial ESL coursework. They expressed concern over the lack of knowledge among many mainstream composition faculty about L2 writing issues (or even awareness that some of their students came from L2 backgrounds). While several respondents noted that some of their composition colleagues had some appreciation of and training in the issues facing L2 students, all respondents felt that such awareness was sorely lacking in faculty across the disciplines. Though a couple of respondents mentioned occasional, poorly attended WAC workshops focused on L2 issues, the clear sense was that there was a long way to go in the preparation of both composition instructors and especially disciplinary faculty to work effectively with L2 students—and worse, that there does not yet appear to be a great interest in or "felt need" for obtaining further training.

My (admittedly limited) investigation into current models of serving the increasingly complex and growing L2 student population at U.S. colleges and universities suggests that while some institutions have developed effective and promising approaches for their specific contexts, many others are just beginning to sort through the practical and philosophical issues that the changing student demographics present.

Going Forward: Guiding Principles and Recommendations

This discussion and the issues raised in the book allow us to articulate a few principles that should guide universities, programs, and individual instructors as they adapt to changing student audiences and/or prepare for such changes in the relatively near future. In outlining these principles, I must acknowledge my indebtedness to two previous documents—*California Pathways* (Browning et al., 2000) and the *CCCC Position Statement on Second Language Writing and Second Language Writers* (CCCC, 2001). The suggestions outlined here are not entirely new but are definitely worth repeating, and they are explicitly related to sections of this book. These principles cover the issues of course options, support services, student placement, assessment, and teacher preparation.

Course Options

Ideally, L2 students should be able to choose between mainstream and designated L2 sections of required writing courses at all levels of the writing curriculum, from remedial through graduate coursework. Designated L2 sections should be taught by well qualified and trained instructors, should carry degree credit that is identical to their mainstream equivalents, and should not include terms such as *ESL* or *Second Language* or *Multilingual* in course titles that will appear on students' transcripts. In addition, designated L2 courses should enroll fewer students than equivalent mainstream sections (see Silva, 1997), and they should include more contact hours (Holten, 2002).

Support Services

It is critical that institutions and especially writing programs develop effective and accessible support services for L2 students. At minimum, every campus should have writing and learning centers that include L2 experts on their staff, and all peer tutors should be carefully trained to work effectively with L2 writers. Some of this necessary training may involve a culture change: Peer writing tutors need to be informed about the language needs of L2 writers and equipped to assist them in these areas (rather than prohibited from doing so, as at Luciana's university), in addition to addressing broader areas of content, organization, and writing process.

Depending on the size of the institution and the relative proportion of L2 students enrolled, programs should also consider providing dedicated tutorial support (e.g., an assigned tutor for every L2 student in a mainstream first-year composition course), small group tutorials on specific writing issues (e.g., grammar editing, vocabulary, or reading skills) or adjunct tutorials (adjunct to writing courses or to general education and major courses popular with L2 students in that setting), and stand-alone elective courses in areas such as grammar, reading, editing strategies, or vocabulary building. Another support option offered by many universities for incoming freshmen and transfer students is a summer bridge program that provides intensive instruction to help L2 and other potentially at-risk students negotiate the transition into college life with a particular focus on academic language and literacy.

Student Identification and Placement

Colleges and universities must develop systems for identifying, appropriately placing, and tracking the progress of L2 students they enroll. Such efforts must go well beyond the simple identification of international students by their visa status and could include language background surveys as part of the admissions process (freshman or transfer) and/or placement testing. Further, individual instructors should gather information about their students at the beginning of each new course, primarily as a way to ensure that they can meet the specialized needs of individual students but also as a back-up to institutional identification and placement processes.

However, such mechanisms should not be used as a means for forcing students into or out of particular classes or discriminating against them in any way. A number of years ago (1992), I was asked to be on a panel of ESL experts speaking to a local group of writing instructors that included high school, community college, and university teachers. We all gave our presentations on how to work with ESL writers in mainstream courses, and then the floor was opened for discussion. The first teacher to raise her hand got right to the point: "I'm really disappointed in this panel. I don't *want* to know how to work with ESL students in my classes. I have enough work to do. I need to know how to get them *out* of my classes!" Heads nodded in agreement around the room. Now, however, it is 2009 (at this moment of writing), and ESL students are far too numerous and diverse to be simply relegated to the ESL program. Few ESL programs at U.S. colleges and universities have enough resources to accommodate all L2 students in their classes, and the students' need for support and sensitivity on the part of their instructors and institutions will continue throughout their undergraduate studies (and graduate, if applicable). Further, not all L2 students want or need to be in ESL classes. The days when composition and disciplinary faculty could claim that working with ESL students is "not their job" are over (if they ever really legitimately existed).

With that said, students should be allowed the freedom to enroll in the various course options available through a process of "directed self-placement" (see Crusan, 2002, 2006, for definition and discussion). Though there is room for debate as to whether students should place themselves as to proficiency levels, it seems fair to state that L2 students should have the right to enroll in mainstream courses if they prefer them to equivalent ESL offerings and, conversely, that students with L2 backgrounds who would feel most comfortable in L2 designated courses should be allowed to enroll in them, even if they appear more assimilated and proficient than other L2 peers. Students should also, of course, be advised as to their options so that their decisions are well informed.

Assessment

Whether assessments are for admissions, placement, evaluation of student progress in specific courses, or graduation requirements, great care should be taken that such assessments are fair to L2 writers: that the topic/subject matter does not pose undue difficulty due to cultural variation, that the language and rhetorical structure of the prompt and task instructions are clear, that adequate time is given for students to do their best work (with perhaps extra time being provided to L2 writers as an appropriate accommodation), and that grading rubrics take L2 writing issues into account. If writing assessments are being scored by non-ESL trained raters, they must receive extra training as to how to fairly score L2 writing, and sample essays used for norming should include proficient texts with observable L2 features (so that raters get the idea that a paper can be otherwise competent but still be "accented"). Ideally, assessment decisions would be made collaboratively between L2 specialists and other faculty through a several-step process so that the fairest outcomes most beneficial to individual students are reached.

Teacher Preparation

This discussion, and those in previous chapters, raises several important and interrelated issues with regard to teacher preparation for working with L2 students (especially writers) in post-secondary instruction.

L2 Specialists

Ideally, L2 specialists, whether they are housed in ESL or writing programs, would have graduate training in both TESOL/applied linguistics and in composition studies. While it is unlikely that many professionals will have the time or means to obtain graduate degrees in both areas, they should pursue a course of cross-training that includes coursework and practical experience in both fields. This might include, for instance, earning a master's in Composition and a TESOL Certificate (or a master's in TESOL and a Composition Certificate), but if such specific options are not available, they should at least take several courses in both areas. It is also to be hoped that, in the future, master's and Ph.D. programs in both Composition and Applied Linguistics might specifically develop tracks or emphases in Second Language Writing that would intentionally prepare instructors and scholars to work in both areas.

The suggestion that TESOL/applied linguistics instructors also obtain training in composition is a bit out of the ordinary (it is more typical to suggest that composition-trained teachers who will work with L2 students take specialized coursework), but it is important because of the widely recognized "disconnect" between the ways in which L2 writing is taught in ESL programs (e.g., language institutes, remedial university courses, and community college courses) and the expectations of the mainstream first-year (and beyond) composition community (see Atkinson & Ramanathan, 1995). If one interviews L2 writing instructors in those specialized contexts, examines their syllabi or their program's curriculum, and compares ESL writing texts designed for pre-college level courses with composition texts designed for mainstream first-year courses, it becomes clear that the goals, approaches, and philosophies behind teaching writing to college and university students can vary greatly between the ESL and composition programs at the same institution. This is especially problematic for students when they encounter these differing approaches as they move from remedial to college-level writing instruction, so it is important for L2 writing teachers at those basic levels to be more aware of and informed about the expectations their students will face in mainstream writing programs so that they (students) can be better prepared for them. Graduate coursework that includes theory and research in teaching composition is a good start in understanding the perspectives of the mainstream composition community.

Mainstream Composition Instructors

Given the increased diversity of student audiences in many settings in the United States, it is also important that all composition instructors receive some specialized training in working with L2 writers (see CCCC, 2001). Such training must go well beyond the token "ESL day" that many graduate courses in teaching college composition include. At a minimum, pre-service instructors should take a course on the theory and practice of teaching L2 writers, a graduate or prerequisite course in linguistics and/or grammar, and obtain practicum or internship experience in working with L2 writers in a tutorial or classroom setting. As for in-service composition instructors and faculty teaching in composition graduate programs, if they did not receive any (or adequate) L2 training in their professional preparation programs, they should look for opportunities to take coursework or attend workshops on working with L2 writers. If none are available, they could do some reading (good entry-level books include Ferris & Hedgcock, 2005; Kroll, 2003; and Leki, 1992) or attend L2-focused presentations at state or national composition conferences.[6]

Faculty in the Disciplines

Composition faculty who serve as WAC specialists or resource people are well aware that it is a challenge to convince colleagues in the disciplines to incorporate or improve writing instruction in their classes. Disciplinary faculty tend to believe that the writing program is supposed to prepare students before they get into their major coursework and do not feel that they have the interest, time, or skills to "teach" writing to their students. Although WAC specialists around the United States and the world have been making inroads for some decades in providing workshops, other resources, and individualized coaching to faculty in the disciplines, it is still an uphill battle in many contexts. The issues surrounding writing in the disciplines are exacerbated further when L2 writing challenges enter the picture. At least composition professionals are passionate about and equipped to teach writing, if not always interested in L2 issues; disciplinary faculty may be motivated neither about writing in general or L2 writers in particular. Nonetheless, WAC specialists should have L2 training and/or should include L2 writing specialists in workshop offerings and one-to-one coaching programs, and L2 specialists should be proactive in offering their expertise and other resources to faculty across the curriculum.

Further Research on Diverse L2 Student Audiences

A number of practical and philosophical ways exist for institutions and programs to better address the needs of an increasingly complex student audience. However, it is only fair to observe that nearly all the suggestions are likely to raise "Yes . . . but . . ." or "That will never work" reactions from experienced (perhaps cynical or jaded) L2 or composition professionals:

- "*Yes*, it would be nice to have designated course offerings for L2 students, *but* there is a strongly held belief in my department that all students should be mainstreamed once they reach the college level."

- "Having assigned tutors for all L2 writers in composition courses *will never work* at my institution. There is not enough money to hire and train the tutors, and the L2 students themselves would balk at having to spend additional time outside of class working on their writing."

- "*Yes*, it would be nice to have writing instructors who are cross-trained in applied linguistics and composition, *but* neither graduate program is going to allow it—that would mean giving up part of their turf."

These pragmatic concerns lead us to the final section, a research agenda that further examines some of the issues raised in this book. Why talk about research in a book that is essentially practical? Empirical investigations are critical because institutional change is more likely if we have actual data to back our assertions, beliefs, and suggestions. Some possible research questions to pursue might include:

- **Populations:** What are the relative proportions of L2 students (and the various sub-groups of L2 students discussed here) in specific regions of the United States or at particular types of institutions (e.g., community colleges in Illinois, the California State University or University of California systems, the CUNY/SUNY systems, private liberal arts colleges, public universities in less diverse states such as Idaho or Utah, etc.)?

- **Pathways:** What kinds of educational/language backgrounds did the L2 students have prior to matriculating at their college/university? Did they graduate from U.S. high schools or in their home country? What kinds of English/literacy/writing instruction did they receive in their prior secondary and post-secondary studies, and how well did it prepare them for their current college/university? What proportion of L2 freshmen or transfer students arrive with college-level language and literacy skills, and what percentage required remedial ESL or writing courses?

- **Programs:** How do specific programs/contexts/systems identify, place, and teach L2 students? For example, what proportion of colleges and universities mainstreams L2 students once they reach the college level, and what proportion provides specialized coursework or designated sections of required courses? What kinds of identification, placement, and assessment mechanisms are used, and how effective are they?

- **Progress:** How are these various students doing—in their writing courses, in their major courses, in completing their degrees? Are they successful or are they struggling? For students who are struggling academically, what is the nature of their struggle (e.g., writing ability, reading fluency and comprehension, listening comprehension, etc.)? How do they feel about their academic experiences—do they feel well prepared and well supported, or underprepared and abandoned to their own resources?

- **Pilots:** If new ideas are implemented, such as separate L2 sections, classes specifically for resident students, adjunct small group tutorials, etc., are they effective? Are they more effective than other or previous approaches?

- **Personnel:** What are the philosophies, approaches, and attitudes of the various faculty groups—L2 specialists, mainstream composition instructors, disciplinary faculty, administrators—toward the needs of L2 students at their institutions? What kinds of knowledge, preparation, and experience about working with L2 students are represented? What kinds of collaboration or training programs can be implemented to provide better information and resources to all faculty, and how can the effectiveness of those cooperative efforts be evaluated?

Such research efforts are important because faculty and administrators who are not L2 specialists may not be as aware of the changes in the student audience and particularly of the issues and challenges those changes raise. Armed with actual data about how many students there are, what their progress/outcomes are, types of programs, support services, and innovations that have been demonstrated to be effective, administrators and teachers may be able to argue successfully for more funds, for different hiring criteria, for pilot versions of courses and programs, and so forth. Further, and importantly, such information will help us be better instructors, course and program developers, teacher educators, textbook authors, resource people for other faculty, and advocates for an often invisible and underserved student audience.

To summarize, although the research cited in this book demonstrates that a great deal has been learned about the different L2 student audiences currently in U.S. colleges and universities, it is also discouraging to note that there is still a long way to go in identifying, placing, and serving these students—and especially in informing and preparing ourselves and other faculty and administrators. However, for those of us who have been working with L2 students at post-secondary institutions for some years, there are reasons to hope: increased awareness in society and in colleges and universities of the growing proportions and complexity of L2 student audiences; a growing sense on the part of more faculty that they need some additional preparation for working with diverse students; cohesive communities of L2 writing professionals within larger organizations such as TESOL and CCCC; and more attention on the part of mainstream composition and disciplinary faculty to the scholarly work of L2 researchers. We still have some distance to travel in our knowledge and especially our implementation of changes, but we (the academic community at large) appear to be headed in the right direction.

QUESTIONS FOR REFLECTION AND DISCUSSION

1. What did you think of the hypothetical suggestions given in the voices of John, Hector, and Luciana? Think of other L2 students whom you know at U.S. colleges or universities. What might they say about their own experiences at their institutions? If you do not know, consider interviewing one or two students, using or adapting the questions in the Appendix at the end of Chapter 3.

2. Some innovative approaches currently being pursued at various institutions were described in this chapter. Are you aware of similar curricular models in your own context or program? Of other models you could add to the list given in this section? Would one or more of the models work in your program, and if not, why do you think so?

3. Another section of this chapter outlined some guiding principles for programs and instruction, based on the observations in this book. Look again at those principles and compare them to the current approaches at your own institution. If you are not sure what the approaches are, consider interviewing a writing program administrator or experienced teacher, using or adapting the questions in the Appendix at the end of this chapter. What changes, if any, do you think your program (or another program with which you are familiar) could or should make?

4. Look at the research questions outlined in the final section of this chapter. Pick one of the sub-headings you find most interesting. Can you think of specific ways you could research one or more of these questions? Can you add other questions or sub-topics to the list?

5. Thinking back on what you have learned about diverse L2 audiences and how post-secondary institutions could/should better understand and address their needs, what surprised you or troubled you the most? If you had the authority and the resources to change something at your current institution or in another program with which you are familiar, what might you change?

CHAPTER ENDNOTES

¹ I did not actually find a Spanish-language equivalent of *SparkNotes* or *Cliffs Notes* for *Huckleberry Finn*. This could be quite a good business idea for someone who is bilingual and literary minded. However, there are indeed both *Cliffs* and *SparkNotes* available for *Huckleberry Finn* (in English) as well as Spanish-language translations of the work itself.

² I had 31 volunteers through the TESOL listserv and 11 returned the survey. Though this was not a large enough return (slightly over 33 percent) to be a "scientific" sample, the comments were detailed and thoughtful, and the respondents represented a broad range of college/university types from all over the United States (and one from Canada).

³ In particular, I am grateful for the insights provided by Mark Roberge of San Francisco State University, who not only filled me in on his program but others in California, Margi Wald of UC Berkeley, and Jan Frodesen of UC Santa Barbara. In addition, due to my own affiliations, I have firsthand knowledge of the programs at CSU Sacramento and UC Davis.

⁴ This model was described by Mark Roberge of SFSU (personal communication, 2008).

⁵ I found the course titles and catalog descriptions on the campus websites of San Francisco State University, UC Berkeley, and UCLA, respectively.

⁶ Both CCCC and TESOL now have interest groups in second language writing (SLW) and thus guaranteed program slots at the annual conferences. It is fair to say, though, that the SLW sessions at CCCC are not well attended by those outside the L2 interest group, leading to a sense of preaching to the choir.

Appendix   Survey Questions

1. Briefly describe your context and location (e.g., "community college in the Minneapolis area").
2. Briefly describe your program (e.g., "we have a separate ESL writing track until the freshman composition level; then students are mainstreamed").
3. If you have separate ESL courses in your program, approximately what percentage of the students in those classes represent each of the audiences described in this chapter? If you are not sure, take your best guess.

International:

Recent Resident Immigrant:

Generation 1.5:

4. At your institution, are any of these "audiences" also found in mainstream (college-level) or basic/developmental (below college-level) writing courses primarily intended for monolingual student writers?
5. Through what process are the L2 students in your context initially placed into writing courses (whether ESL, mainstream, or basic)? Can they change courses if they do not agree with their placement? Generally speaking, how satisfactory or effective do you think these placement mechanisms are?
6. Considering ESL writing courses specifically, are students from two or all three of the audiences taught together in the same course(s)? Are there any separate offerings for specific groups (e.g., a dedicated section for international students?) If so, do you find this to be an effective model for instruction? What problems or concerns (if any) do you have with keeping all L2 writers together, regardless of their differences in background?
7. If you have taught any or all of these student audiences in your own courses, what do you see as the primary needs or struggles of each group (as to various academic literacy skills in particular, but any other issues you think relevant, such as cultural adjustment, listening comprehension, etc.)?

International:

Recent Resident Immigrant:

Generation 1.5:

8. Do you feel that you yourself were adequately trained (either pre- or in-service) to identify and respond to the needs of diverse audiences of L2 student writers? If yes, what helped you? If no, what kinds of coursework or other preparation do you wish you had had (or could have now)?
9. If you have been teaching L2 writing for awhile (say ten years or longer), comment on whether and how your perceptions and teaching practices have changed with regard to serving the different audiences.
10. Besides the writing courses themselves, what other types of support services are available to L2 writers in your context? Do you feel that they are adequate and effective? Why or why not?

Appendix (continued)

11. In your opinion or observation, are "mainstream" composition instructors (i.e., those teaching courses *not* designated for L2 writers) aware of the needs of linguistically diverse student audiences and equipped to meet them? If yes, what types of training and support do they/ have they received? If no, what concerns do you have about their preparation and aware-ness? For this question, consider also instructors or tutors in campus writing or learning centers or other support programs.

12. In your opinion or observation, are faculty across the disciplines aware of the needs of linguistically diverse student audiences and equipped to meet them? If yes, what types of training and support do they/have they received? If no, what concerns do you have about their preparation and awareness?

13. If money, resources, and bureaucracy were not barriers, what changes would you suggest or make in the way(s) your institution serves L2 writers?

Any other comments you would like to add?

Postscript: A Plea for Greater Collaboration among Writing Professionals

> As important as ESL faculty are in serving ESL students, they cannot begin to do the job by themselves.
> —Browning et al. (2000), *California Pathways*, p. 52

As I worked on this book, I became increasingly aware that the issues raised are important to a readership far larger than simply the community of ESL professionals. As I hope this book has demonstrated, L2 students need the support of the entire academic community throughout their years of education. Yet there is still a discouraging lack of communication among composition professionals (L1 and L2) in post-secondary contexts.

Although there is now a second language writing Special Interest Group (SIG) in CCCC, only a relative handful of the L2 writing SIG members attended CCCC in 2008 because it was scheduled in direct conflict with TESOL, which also has a second language writing interest section (IS). More disheartening than this scheduling conflict was the fact that the L2 writing sessions at CCCC were generally poorly attended, with some fine panels drawing audiences in the single digits. Though L2 professionals have made inroads at the organizational level by having a SIG established and by getting more presentations scheduled, the felt need to learn about L2 writing had apparently not spread to the average composition professionals attending the conference. Similarly, as I browsed the book exhibits, I discovered two things: (1) several popular books on teaching L2 writing were not even on display, although their publishers had booths; and (2) new edited collections on important topics such as teacher response and assessment had no chapters written by L2 professionals and/or focused on serving a broad and diverse student audience.

To mainstream composition instructors or administrators or pre-service instructors who may be reading this book, I offer you three challenges:

1. Get to know our scholarship. If you are doing a literature search or review on a specific composition topic, look in L2 journals and books[1] as well as your own publications. You may be surprised to find that L2 researchers are looking at some of the same issues and in some interesting ways.

2. Commit yourself to learning more about L2 students, their needs, and approaches that have been used to help them develop advanced academic literacy skills. There are several specific suggestions along these lines in Chapters 5–6.

3. A further challenge is more philosophical and cultural: Do not dismiss L2 students as being "not your job," and do not dismiss L2 writing professionals as being "only interested in grammar." Both generalizations are unhelpful.

As for L2 writing professionals, I would offer a similar challenge, and I would aim it at myself first. Recently I was assembling a file of my publications going back about fifteen years, and I noticed an interesting change. In my early articles, most or all of the citations in my list of references came from L1 composition sources. There was a good reason for this: In the early 1990s, there had still been relatively little published about L2 writing or writers. However, this pattern changed dramatically with the inception of the *Journal of Second Language Writing* in 1992, not to mention a mini-explosion of books and collections on general or specific L2 writing topics. As a result, I noticed that in my more recent publications, I was citing exclusively L2 sources. I need to remind or challenge myself to read more broadly, to attend the "mainstream" presentations at CCCC as well as the L2 sessions, and, most important, to maintain good lines of two-way communication with my mainstream composition colleagues.

I have found that L2 writing specialists as a group have a bit of a chip on their shoulders. They have felt ignored, disrespected, and marginalized by colleagues in English departments and composition programs, and they feel both personally resentful about ways they have been dismissed and strongly protective of the ESL students they serve. Recently I was at a training session for composition instructors in my department, and there was a heated debate about whether L2 writers' texts in large-scale assessments should be scored only by trained L2 instructors or by all raters. One L2 instructor spoke up strongly: "I got a master's degree in TESOL, and it's an insult to my training to say that anyone is qualified to assess L2 writing." An L1 instructor fired back that she felt insulted that others might think she wasn't smart enough or fair enough to learn to assess L2 writing accurately. Talking privately later about this same assessment issue, several L2 instructors grumbled, "Why can't the composition people stay out of it and leave the ESL students to the professionals?"

I believe that such a turf mentality is counterproductive. As I have already noted, in many settings, we are all teaching the same (or similar) student populations, and we need to be collaborating, not competing. There are some specific ways, large and small, that programs and individual faculty might intentionally pursue more productive partnerships:

1. At the programmatic level, administrators should assess whether having ESL programs separate from other writing programs might be counterproductive.

2. If possible, L1 and L2 composition faculty should serve together on program committees, attend the same orientations and training sessions, and assess writing together.

3. L1 and L2 faculty should collaborate on research projects, grant proposals, program development, and course design.

4. L1 and L2 composition instructors should observe each other's classes, share teaching resources (perhaps on a program website), and give each other suggestions about additional materials (books, new journal articles, local/regional workshops, conferences) that could benefit the whole program.

It is time—in fact it is well past time—for writing professionals to move beyond, or close entirely, the "disciplinary division of labor" that Matsuda (1999) wrote of nearly a decade ago. The future success of writing programs and of L2 students in post-secondary contexts depends on the development and implementation of productive new paradigms. Finally, I would add, it is the responsibility, even the obligation, of those of us who call ourselves L2 specialists to take the initiative and lead the way.

POSTSCRIPT ENDNOTE

[1] For book ideas, see the Endnotes in Chapter 5. For journals, start with the *Journal of Second Language Writing* and the *TESOL Quarterly*, both American publications that are widely available in university libraries.

REFERENCES

Adamson, H.D. (1993). *Academic competence. Theory and classroom practice: Preparing ESL students for content courses*. New York: Longman.

Aebersold, J., & Field, M. (1997). *From reader to reading teacher: Issues and strategies for second language classrooms*. Cambridge, UK: Cambridge University Press.

Arndt, V. (1993). Response to writing: Using feedback to inform the writing process. In M. N. Brock & L. Walters (Eds.), *Teaching composition around the Pacific Rim: Politics & pedagogy* (pp. 90–116). Clevedon, UK: Multilingual Matters.

Atkinson, D., & Ramanathan, V. (1995). Cultures of writing: An ethnographic comparison of L1 and L2 university writing/language programs. *TESOL Quarterly, 29*(3), 539–568.

Bates, L., Lane, J., & Lange, E. (1993). *Writing clearly: Responding to student writing*. Boston: Heinle & Heinle.

Belcher, D. (1999). Authentic interaction in a virtual classroom: Leveling the playing field in a graduate seminar. *Computers and Composition, 16*, 253–267.

Benson, B., Deming, M. P., Denzer, D., & Valeri-Gold, M. (1992). A combined basic writing/English as a second language class: Melting pot or mishmash? *Journal of Basic Writing, 11*(1), 58–74.

Biber, D. (1988). *Variation across speech and writing*. New York: Cambridge University Press.

———. (2006). *University language*. Amsterdam: John Benjamins.

Birch, B. M. (2007). *English L2 reading: Getting to the bottom* (2nd ed.). Mahwah, NJ: Lawrence Erlbaum.

Bitchener, J. (2008, in press). Evidence in support of written corrective feedback. *Journal of Second Language Writing, 17*, 102–118.

Bitchener, J., & Knoch, U. (2008). The value of written corrective feedback for migrant and international students. *Language Teaching Research, 12*, 409–431.

Bitchener, J., Young, S., & Cameron, D. (2005). The effect of different types of corrective feedback on ESL student writing. *Journal of Second Language Writing, 9*, 227–258.

Blanton, L.L. (1999). Classroom instruction and language minority students: On teaching to "smarter" readers and writers. In L. Harklau, K. Losey, & M. Siegal (Eds.), *Generation 1.5 meets college composition: Issues in the teaching of writing to U.S.-educated learners of ESL* (pp. 119–142). Mahwah, NJ: Lawrence Erlbaum.

———. (2005). Student, interrupted: A tale of two would-be writers. *Journal of Second Language Writing, 14*(2), 105–121.

Blanton, L.L., & Kroll, B. (2002). *ESL composition tales: Reflections on Teaching*. Ann Arbor: University of Michigan Press.

Bosher, S., & Rowecamp, J. (1998). The refugee/immigrant in higher education: The role of educational background. *College ESL, 8*(1), 23–42.

Braine, G. (1996). ESL students in first-year writing courses: ESL versus mainstream classes. *Journal of Second Language Writing, 5,* 91–107.

Browning, G., Brinton, D., Ching, R., Dees, R., Dunlap, S., Erickson, M., Garlow, K., Manson, M., & Sasser, L. (2000). *California pathways: The second language student in public high schools, colleges, and universities*. Sacramento: California Community Colleges Chancellor's Office. Retrieved from www.catesol.org

Bruce, S. (2004). ESL students share their writing center experiences. In S. Bruce & B. Rafoth (Eds.), *ESL writers: A guide for writing center tutors* (pp. 149–161). Portsmouth, NH: Boynton/Cook Heinemann.

Bruce, S. & Rafoth, B. (Eds.). (2004). *ESL writers: A guide for writing center tutors*. Portsmouth, NH: Boynton/Cook Heinemann.

Byrd, P., & Bunting, J. (2008). Myth 3: Where grammar is concerned, one size fits all. In J. Reid (Ed.), *Writing myths: Applying second language research to classroom teaching* (pp. 42–69). Ann Arbor: University of Michigan Press.

California Content Standards for English Language Arts. (n.d.). Retrieved Dec. 28, 2008, from www.sdcoe.k12.ca.us/SCORE/stand/std.html

California State University Expository Reading and Writing Task Force (2008). *Expository reading and writing course: Semester one and semester two*. Long Beach: California State University.

Casanave, C.P. (2004). *Controversies in second language writing: Dilemmas and decisions in research and instruction*. Ann Arbor: University of Michigan Press.

Chiang, Y-S., & Schmida, M. (1999). Language identity and language ownership: Linguistic conflicts of first-year university writing students. In L. Harklau, K. Losey, & M. Siegal (Eds.), *Generation 1.5 meets college composition: Issues in the teaching of writing to U.S.-educated learners of ESL* (pp. 81–96). Mahwah, NJ: Lawrence Erlbaum.

Cobb, T. (2007). *The Compleat Lexical Tutor*. Retrieved Dec. 28, 2008, from www.lextutor.ca

Collier, V. (1987). Age and rate of acquisition of second languages for academic purposes. *TESOL Quarterly, 21*(4), 617–641.

———. (1989). How long? A synthesis of research on academic achievement in a second language. *TESOL Quarterly, 23,* 509–531.

Conference on College Composition and Communication (CCCC). (2001). *Statement on second language writing and writers*. Retrieved Oct. 25, 2007, from www.ncte.org/cccc/resources/123794.htm

Connor, U. (1996). *Contrastive rhetoric: Cross-cultural aspects of second-language writing*. New York: Cambridge University Press.

————. (2003). Changing currents in contrastive rhetoric: Implications for teaching and research. In B. Kroll (Ed.), *Exploring the dynamics of second language writing* (pp. 218–241). Cambridge, UK: Cambridge University Press.

Connor, U., & Asenavage, K. (1994). Peer response groups in ESL writing classes: How much impact on revision? *Journal of Second Language Writing, 3,* 257–276.

Connors, R.J. (1993). The new abolitionism: Toward a historical background. In J. Petraglia (Ed.), *Reconceiving writing, rethinking writing instruction* (pp. 3–26). Mahwah, NJ: Lawrence Erlbaum.

Conrad, S. (2008). Myth 6: Corpus-based research is too complicated to be useful for writing teachers. In J. Reid (Ed.), *Writing myths: Applying second language research to classroom teaching* (pp. 115–139). Ann Arbor: University of Michigan Press.

Conrad, S.M., & Goldstein, L.M. (1999). ESL student revision after teacher-written comments: Text, contexts, and individuals. *Journal of Second Language Writing, 8,* 147–180.

Costino, K.A., & Hyon, S. (2007). "A class for students like me": Reconsidering relationships among identity labels, residency status, and students' preferences for mainstream or multilingual composition. *Journal of Second Language Writing, 16*(2), 63–81.

Coxhead, A. (2000). A new academic word list. *TESOL Quarterly, 34*(2), 213–238.

————. (2006). *Essentials of teaching academic vocabulary.* Boston: Houghton Mifflin.

Coxhead, A., & Byrd, P. (2007). Preparing writing teachers to teach the vocabulary and grammar of academic prose. *Journal of Second Language Writing, 16*(3), 129–147.

Crusan, D. (2002). An assessment of ESL writing placement assessment. *Assessing Writing, 8,* 17–30.

————. (2006). The politics of implementing online directed self-placement for second language writers. In P.K. Matsuda, C. Ortmeier-Hooper, & X. You (Eds.), *The politics of second language writing: In search of the promised land* (pp. 205–221). West Lafayette, IN: Parlor Press.

Cummins, J. (1979). Cognitive/academic language proficiency, linguistic interdependence, the optimal age question and some other matters. *Working Papers on Bilingualism, 19,* 197–205.

Cummins, J., & Swain, M. (1986). *Bilingualism in education: Aspects of theory, research, and practice.* New York: Longman.

Day, R. R., & Bamford, J. (1998). *Extensive reading in the second language classroom.* New York: Cambridge University Press.

Destandau, N., & Wald, M. (2002). Promoting Generation 1.5 learners' academic literacy and autonomy: Contributions from the learning center. *CATESOL Journal, 14*(1), 207–234.

Doughty, C., & Williams, J. (1998). *Focus on form in second language acquisition.* New York: Cambridge University Press.

Dudley-Evans, T. (1994). Variations in the discourse patterns favoured by different disciplines and their pedagogical implications. In J. Flowerdew (Ed.), *Academic listening: Research perspectives* (pp. 146–158). Cambridge, UK: Cambridge University Press.

Edlund, J.R. (2003). Non-native speakers of English. In I.L. Clark (Ed.), *Concepts in composition: Theory and practice in the teaching of writing* (pp. 363–412). Mahwah, NJ: Lawrence Erlbaum.

Ellis, R. (2004). The definition and measurement of L2 explicit knowledge. *Language Learning, 52*(2), 227–275.

Ellis, R., Loewen, S., & Erlam, R. (2006). Implicit and explicit corrective feedback and the acquisition of L2 grammar. *Studies in Second Language Acquisition, 28*, 339–368.

Ellis, R., Sheen, Y., Murakami, M., & Takashima, H. (2008). The effects of focused and unfocused written corrective feedback in an English as a Foreign Language context. *System, 36*, 353–371.

Eskey, D.E. (1983). Meanwhile, back in the real world . . . : Accuracy and fluency in second language teaching. *TESOL Quarterly, 17*(2), 315–323.

Ferris, D.R. (1995). Teaching students to self-edit. *TESOL Journal 4*(4), 18–22.

———. (1997). The influence of teacher commentary on student revision. *TESOL Quarterly, 31*, 315–339.

———. (1998). Students' views of academic aural/oral skills: A comparative needs analysis. *TESOL Quarterly, 32*(2), 289–318.

———. (1999). One size does not fit all: Response and revision issues for immigrant student writers. In L. Harklau, K. Losey, & M. Siegel (Eds.), *Generation 1.5 meets college composition: Issues in the teaching of writing to U.S.-educated learners of ESL* (pp. 143–157). Mahwah, NJ: Lawrence Erlbaum.

———. (2001). Teaching writing for academic purposes. In J. Flowerdew & M. Peacock (Eds.), *Research perspectives on English for academic purposes* (pp. 298–314). Cambridge, UK: Cambridge University Press.

———. (2002). *Treatment of error in second language student writing*. Ann Arbor: University of Michigan Press.

———. (2003). *Response to student writing*. Mahwah, NJ: Lawrence Erlbaum.

———. (2004) The "grammar correction" debate in L2 writing: Where are we, and where do we go from here? (and what do we do in the meantime . . . ?). *Journal of Second Language Writing, 13*, 49–62.

———. (2006). Does error feedback help student writers? New evidence on the short- and long-term effects of written error correction. In K. Hyland & F. Hyland (Eds.), *Feedback in second language writing* (pp. 81–104). Cambridge, UK: Cambridge University Press.

———. (2008). Myth 5: Students must learn to correct all their writing errors. In J. Reid (Ed.), *Writing myths: Applying second language research to classroom teaching* (pp. 90–114). Ann Arbor: University of Michigan Press.

Ferris, D.R., & Hedgcock, J.S. (2005). *Teaching ESL composition* (2nd Ed.). Mahwah, NJ: Lawrence Erlbaum.

Ferris, D., Pezone, S., Tade, C., & Tinti, S. (1997). Teacher commentary on student writing: Descriptions and implications. *Journal of Second Language Writing, 6*, 155–182.

Ferris, D.R., & Roberts, B.J. (2001). Error feedback in L2 writing classes: How explicit does it need to be? *Journal of Second Language Writing, 10,* 161–184.

Ferris, D.R., & Tagg, T. (1996a). Academic listening/speaking tasks for ESL students: Problems, suggestions, and implications. *TESOL Quarterly, 30*(2), 297–320.

————. (1996b). Academic oral communication needs of EAP learners: What subject-matter instructors actually require. *TESOL Quarterly, 30*(1), 31–58.

Flowerdew, J. (Ed.) (1994). *Academic listening: Research perspectives.* Cambridge, UK: Cambridge University Press.

Folse, K.S. (2004). *Vocabulary myths: Applying second language research to classroom teaching.* Ann Arbor: University of Michigan Press.

————. (2008). Myth 1: Teaching vocabulary is not the writing teacher's job. In J. Reid (Ed.), *Writing myths: Applying second language research to classroom teaching* (pp. 1–17). Ann Arbor: University of Michigan Press.

Friedrich, P. (2006). Assessing the needs of linguistically diverse first-year students: Bringing together and telling apart international ESL, resident ESL and monolingual basic writers. *Writing Program Administration, 30,* 15–35.

Frodesen, J. (2002). At what price success? The academic writing development of a Generation 1.5 "Latecomer." *CATESOL Journal, 14*(1), 191–206.

Frodesen, J. & Starna, N. (1999). Distinguishing incipient and functional bilingual writers: Assessment and instructional insights gained through second-language writer profiles. In L. Harklau, K. Losey, & M. Siegal (Eds.), *Generation 1.5 meets college composition: Issues in the teaching of writing to U.S.-educated learners of ESL* (pp. 61–80). Mahwah, NJ: Lawrence Erlbaum.

Goen, S., Porter, P., Swanson, D., & vanDommelen, D. (2002). Working with Generation 1.5 students and their teachers: ESL meets composition. *CATESOL Journal, 14*(1), 131–171.

Goldstein, L., & Conrad, S. (1990). Student input and the negotiation of meaning in ESL writing conferences. *TESOL Quarterly, 24,* 443–460.

Goldstein, L.M. (2005). *Teacher written commentary in second language writing classrooms.* Ann Arbor: University of Michigan Press.

Grabe, W., & Stoller, F. (2002). *Teaching and researching reading.* Harlow, UK: Longman/ Pearson Education.

Hamp-Lyons, L. (2003). Writing teachers as assessors of writing. In B. Kroll (Ed.), *Exploring the dynamics of second language writing* (pp. 162–189). Cambridge, UK: Cambridge University Press.

Harklau, L. (1994). ESL versus mainstream classes: Contrasting L2 learning environments. *TESOL Quarterly, 28*(2), 241–272.

————. (2000). From the "good kids" to the "worst": Representations of English language learners across educational settings. *TESOL Quarterly, 34,* 35–67.

————. (2003). Generation 1.5 students and college writing. *ERIC Digest,* EDO-FL-03-05 (October 2003). Retrieved July 9, 2007, from www.cal.org/ericcll

Harklau, L., Losey, K. & Siegal, M. (Eds.). (1999). *Generation 1.5 meets college composition: Issues in the teaching of writing to U.S.-educated learners of ESL.* Mahwah, NJ: Lawrence Erlbaum.

Harklau, L., Siegal, M., & Losey, K. (1999). Linguistically diverse students and college writing: What is equitable and appropriate. In L. Harklau, K. Losey, & M. Siegal (Eds.), *Generation 1.5 meets college composition: Issues in the teaching of writing to U.S.-educated learners of ESL* (pp. 1–14). Mahwah, NJ: Lawrence Erlbaum.

Hartman, B., & Tarone, E. (1999). Preparation for college writing: Teachers talk about writing instruction for Southeast Asian American students in secondary school. In L. Harklau, K. Losey, & M. Siegal (Eds.), *Generation 1.5 meets college composition: Issues in the teaching of writing to U.S.-educated learners of ESL* (pp. 99–118). Mahwah, NJ: Lawrence Erlbaum.

Hedgcock, J.S., & Ferris, D.R. (2009). *Teaching readers of English: Students, texts, and contexts.* New York: Routledge/Taylor & Francis.

Hinds, J. (1987). Reader vs. writer responsibility: A new typology. In U. Connor & R.B. Kaplan (Eds.), *Writing across languages: Analysis of L2 text* (pp. 141–152). Reading, MA: Addison-Wesley.

Hinkel, E. (2002). *Second language writers' text.* Mahwah, NJ: Lawrence Erlbaum.

———. (2004). *Teaching academic ESL writing: Practical techniques in vocabulary and grammar.* Mahwah, NJ: Lawrence Erlbaum.

Hirvela, A. (2004). *Connecting reading and writing in second language writing instruction.* Ann Arbor: University of Michigan Press.

Holten, C. (2002). Charting new territory: Creating an interdepartmental course for Generation 1.5 writers. *CATESOL Journal, 14*(1), 173–189.

Horowitz, D.M. (1986). What professors actually require: Academic tasks for the ESL classroom. *TESOL Quarterly, 20*(3), 445–462.

Hudson, T. (2007). *Teaching second language readers.* Oxford, UK: Oxford University Press.

Hyland, K. (2002). *Teaching and researching writing.* London: Longman.

Hyland, K., & Hyland, F. (Eds.) (2006). *Feedback in second language writing.* Cambridge, UK: Cambridge University Press.

Institute of International Education (IIE). (2007). Open Doors 2007: International students in the U.S. *HE Network* (Nov. 12, 2007). Retrieved Dec. 15, 2007, from http://opendoors.iienetwork.org

James, D.C.S. (1997). Coping with a new society: The psychosocial problems of immigrant youth. *Journal of School Health, 67*(3), 98–101.

Jensen, L. (1986). Advanced reading skills in a comprehensive course. In F. Dubin, D.E. Eskey, & W. Grabe (Eds.), *Teaching second language reading for academic purposes* (pp. 103–124). Reading, MA: Addison-Wesley.

Johns, A.M. (1997). *Text, role, and context.* Cambridge, UK: Cambridge University Press.

———. (1999). Opening our doors: Applying socioliterate approaches to language minority classrooms. In L. Harklau, K. Losey, M. Siegal (Eds.), *Generation 1.5 meets college composition: Issues in the teaching of writing to U.S.-educated learners of ESL* (pp. 159–171). Mahwah, NJ: Lawrence Erlbaum.

Kaplan, R.B. (1966). Cultural thought patterns in intercultural education. *Language Learning, 16*, 1–20.

Kern, R. (2000). *Notions of literacy*. In R. Kern (Ed.), *Literacy and language teaching* (pp. 13–14). New York: Oxford University Press.

Kobayashi, H., & Rinnert, C. (2002). High school student perceptions of first language literacy instruction: Implications for second language writing. *Journal of Second Language Writing, 11*(2), 91–116.

Koda, K. (2004). *Insights into second language reading: A cross-linguistic approach.* Cambridge, UK: Cambridge University Press.

Krashen, S.D. (1982). *Principles and practice in second language acquisition.* New York: Prentice Hall.

———. (2004). *The power of reading* (2nd ed.). Portsmouth, NH: Heinemann.

Krashen, S.D., & Terrell, T. (1983). *The natural approach: Language acquisition in the classroom.* San Francisco: Alemany Press.

Kroll, B. (1990a). The rhetoric-syntax split: Designing a curriculum for ESL students. *Journal of Basic Writing, 9*(1), 40–55.

———. (1990b). What does time buy? ESL student performance on home versus class compositions. In B. Kroll (Ed.), *Second language writing: Research insights for the classroom* (pp. 140–154). New York: Cambridge University Press.

———. (Ed.). (2003). *Exploring the dynamics of second language writing.* New York: Cambridge University Press.

———. (2006). Toward a promised land of writing: At the intersection of hope and reality. In P.K. Matsuda, C. Ortmeier-Hooper, & X. You (Eds.), *The politics of second language writing: In search of the promised land* (pp. 297–305). West Lafayette, IN: Parlor Press.

Lane, J., & Lange, E. (1999). *Writing clearly* (2nd ed.). Boston: Heinle & Heinle.

Lay, N.D.S., Carro, G., Tien, S., Niemann, T.C., & Leong, S. (1999). Connections: High school to college. In L. Harklau, K. Losey, & M. Siegal (Eds.), *Generation 1.5 meets college composition: Issues in the teaching of writing to U.S.-educated learners of ESL* (pp. 175–190). Mahwah, NJ: Lawrence Erlbaum.

Leki, I. (1992). *Understanding ESL writers.* Portsmouth, NH: Boynton/Cook Heinemann.

———. (1993). Reciprocal themes in ESL reading and writing. In J. Carson & I. Leki (Eds.), *Reading in the composition classroom: Second language perspectives* (pp. 9–32). Boston: Heinle & Heinle.

———. (1995). Coping strategies of ESL students in writing tasks across the curriculum. *TESOL Quarterly, 29*, 235–260.

————. (1999). "Pretty much I screwed up": Ill-served needs of a permanent resident. In L. Harklau, K. Losey, & M. Siegal (Eds), *Generation 1.5 meets college composition: Issues in the teaching of writing to U.S.-educated learners of ESL* (pp. 17–44). Mahwah, NJ: Lawrence Erlbaum.

————. (2004). Foreword. In S. Bruce & B. Rafoth (Eds.), *ESL writers: A guide for writing center tutors* (pp. xi–xii). Portsmouth, NH: Boynton/Cook Heinemann.

Leki, I., Cumming, A., & Silva, T. (2006). Second-language composition: Teaching and learning. In P. Smagorinsky (Ed.), *Research on composition: Multiple perspectives on two decades of change* (pp. 141–169). New York: Teachers College Press.

Linville, C. (2004). Editing line by line. In S. Bruce & B. Rafoth (Eds.), *ESL writers: A guide for writing center tutors* (pp. 84–93). Portsmouth, NH: Boynton/Cook Heinemann.

Liu, J., & Hansen, J. (2002). *Peer response in second language writing classrooms.* Ann Arbor: University of Michigan Press.

Locke, M. (2007, July 20). Immigrants loom large in UC system. *Sacramento Bee*, pp. A3–4.

Lynch, T. (1994). Training lecturers for international audiences. In J. Flowerdew (Ed.), *Academic Listening: Research Perspectives* (pp. 269–289). Cambridge, UK: Cambridge University Press.

Mason, A. (1994). By dint of: Student and lecturer perceptions of lecture comprehension strategies in first-term graduate study. In J. Flowerdew (Ed.), *Academic Listening: Research Perspectives* (pp. 199–218). Cambridge, UK: Cambridge University Press.

Matsuda, P. K. (1999). Composition studies and ESL writing: A disciplinary division of labor. *College Composition and Communication, 50,* 699–721.

————. (2003a). Basic writing and second language writers: Toward an inclusive definition. *Journal of Basic Writing, 22*(2), 67–89.

————. (2003b). Process and post-process: A discursive history. *Journal of Second Language Writing, 12*(1), 65–83.

————. (2006a). The myth of linguistic homogeneity in U.S. college composition. *College English, 68*(6), 637–651.

————. (2006b). Second-language writing in the twentieth century: A situated historical perspective. In P.K. Matsuda, M. Cox, J. Jordan, & C. Ortmeier-Hooper (Eds.), *Second-language writing in the composition classroom* (pp. 14–30). Boston: Bedford/ St. Martin's.

————. (2008). Myth 8: International and U.S. resident ESL writers cannot be taught in the same class. In J. Reid (Ed.), *Writing myths: Applying second language research to classroom teaching* (pp. 159–176). Ann Arbor: University of Michigan Press.

Matsuda, P. K., Canagarajah, A. S., Harklau, L., Hyland, K., & Warschauer, M. (2003). Changing currents in second language writing research: A colloquium. *Journal of Second Language Writing, 12*(2), 151–179.

Matsuda, P.K., Cox, M., Jordan, J., & Ortmeier-Hooper, C. (2006a). Introduction. In P.K. Matsuda, M. Cox, J. Jordan, & C. Ortmeier-Hooper (Eds.), *Second-language writing in the composition classroom* (pp. 1–4). Boston: Bedford/St. Martin's.

———. (Eds.). (2006b). *Second-language writing in the composition classroom*. Boston: Bedford/St. Martin's.

Matsuda, P. K., & Matsuda, A. (2009). Erasure of resident ESL writers. In M. Roberge, M. Siegal, & L. Harklau (Eds.), *Generation 1.5 in college composition: Teaching academic writing to U.S.-educated learners of ESL* (pp. 50–64). New York: Routledge/Taylor & Francis.

Matsuda, P. K., & Silva, T. (1999). Cross-cultural composition: Mediated integration of U.S. and international students. *Composition Studies, 27*(1), 15–30.

McKay, S.L., & Wong, S.C. (Eds.). (2000). *New immigrants in the United States: Readings for second language educators*. Cambridge, UK: Cambridge University Press.

McNamara, T.F. (1996). *Measuring second language performance*. London: Longman.

Muchisky, D., & Tangren, N. (1999). Immigrant student performance in an academic intensive English program. In L. Harklau, K. Losey, & M. Siegal (Eds.), *Generation 1.5 meets college composition: Issues in the teaching of writing to U.S.-educated learners of ESL* (pp. 211–234). Mahwah, NJ: Lawrence Erlbaum.

Murphy, J. (2006). *Essentials of teaching academic oral communication*. Boston: Houghton Mifflin.

Murphy, J., & Byrd, P. (Eds.). (2001). *Understanding the courses we teach: Local perspectives on English language teaching*. Ann Arbor: University of Michigan Press.

Nation, I.S.P. (2001). *Learning vocabulary in another language*. Cambridge, UK: Cambridge University Press.

Nero, S. (1997). English is my native language…or so I believe. *TESOL Quarterly 31*(3), 585–593.

Newkirk, T. (1995). The writing conference as performance. *Research in the Teaching of English, 29*(2), 193–215.

Olsen, L. (1997). *Made in America: Immigrant students in our public schools*. New York: New Press.

Ortmeier-Hooper, C. (2008). English may be my second language—but I'm not "ESL." *College Composition and Communication, 59*(3), 389–419.

Paral, R. (2008). *Integration potential of California's immigrants and their children*. Sebastapol, CA: Grantmakers Concerned with Immigrants and Refugees. Report cited in S. Ferriss, *Sacramento Bee*, April 29, p. A3. Report retrieved April 30, 2008, from www.sacbee.com/links

Park, K. (1999). "I really do feel I'm 1.5": The construction of self and community by young Korean Americans. *Amerasia Journal, 25*(1) 139–163.

Parsad, B., & Lewis, L. (2000). Remedial education at degree-granting postsecondary institutions in Fall 2000. *Education Statistics Quarterly, 5*(4). Retrieved Sept. 25, 2007, from http://nces.ed.gov/programs/quarterly/Vol_5/5_4/4_4.asp

Patthey-Chavez, G.G., & Ferris, D.R. (1997). Writing conferences and the weaving of multi-voiced texts in college composition. *Research in the Teaching of English, 31,* 51–90.

Pienemann, M., & Johnson, M. (1987). Factors influencing the development of language proficiency. In D. Nunan (Ed.), *Applying second language acquisition research* (pp. 45–141). Adelaide, Australia: National Curriculum Resource Centre.

Pope, J. (2007, July 19). College for all: State community campuses get students in school, not always out. *The Davis Enterprise,* pp. A1, A10.

Purves, A. (1992). Reflection on research and assessment in written composition. *Research in the Teaching of English, 26,* 108–122.

Raimes, A. (1985). What unskilled ESL students do as they write: A classroom study of composing. *TESOL Quarterly, 19,* 225–258.

———. (1991). Out of the woods: Emerging traditions in the teaching of writing. *TESOL Quarterly, 25,* 407–430.

Reid, J. (1994). Responding to ESL students' texts: The myths of appropriation. *TESOL Quarterly, 28,* 273–292.

———. (1997). Which non-native speaker: Differences between international students and U.S. resident (language minority) students. *New Directions for Teaching and Learning, 70,* 17–27.

———. (1998/2006b). "Eye" learners and "ear" learners: Identifying the language needs of international students and US resident writers. In P.K. Matsuda, M. Cox, J. Jordan, & C. Ortmeier-Hooper (Eds.), *Second-language writing in the composition classroom* (pp. 76–88). Boston: Bedford/St. Martin's.

———. (2006a). *Essentials of teaching academic writing.* Boston: Houghton Mifflin.

———. (Ed.). (2008). *Writing myths: Applying second language research to classroom teaching.* Ann Arbor: University of Michigan Press.

Reid, J., & Kroll, B. (1995). Designing and assessing effective classroom writing assignments for NES and ESL students. *Journal of Second Language Writing, 4*(1), 17–41.

Reynolds, D. (2005). Linguistic correlates of second language literacy development: Evidence from middle-grade learner essays. *Journal of Second Language Writing, 14*(1), 19–45.

Robb, T. (2001). "Extensive reading" for Japanese English majors. In J. Murphy & P. Byrd (Eds.), *Understanding the courses we teach: Local perspectives on English language teaching* (pp. 218–235). Ann Arbor: University of Michigan Press.

Robb, T., Ross, S., & Shortreed, I. (1986). Salience of feedback on error and its effect on EFL writing quality. *TESOL Quarterly, 20,* 83–93.

Roberge, M.M. (2002). California's Generation 1.5 immigrants: What experiences, characteristics, and needs do they bring to our English classes? *CATESOL Journal, 14*(1), 107–129.

Rodby, J. (1999). Contingent literacy: The social construction of writing for nonnative English-speaking college freshman. In L. Harklau, K. Losey, & M. Siegal (Eds.), *Generation 1.5 meets college composition: Issues in the teaching of writing to U.S.-educated learners of ESL* (pp. 45–60). Mahwah, NJ: Lawrence Erlbaum.

Roy, A. (1988). ESL concerns for writing program administrators. *Writing Program Administration, 11,* 17–28.

Rumbaut, R.G. & Ima, K. (1988). *The adaptation of Southeast Asian refugee youth: A comparative study.* Final Report to the U.S. Department of Health and Human Services, Office of Refugee Resettlement, Washington, D.C.: U.S. Department of Health and Human Services. San Diego: San Diego State University. (ERIC Document Reproduction Service No. ED299372)

Scarcella, R.C. (1996). Secondary education in California and second language research. *CATESOL Journal, 9*(1), 129–152.

———. (2003). *Accelerating academic English: A focus on the English learner.* Oakland: University of California.

Schachter, J.L. (1974). An error in error analysis. *Language Learning, 24*(2), 205–214.

Schleppegrell, M. J. (2004). *The language of schooling: A functional linguistics perspective.* Mahwah, NJ: Lawrence, Erlbaum.

Schleppegrell, M. J., & Colombi, M. C. (Eds.). (2002). *Developing advanced literacy in first and second languages.* Mahwah, NJ: Lawrence Erlbaum.

Schmitt, N. (2000). *Vocabulary in language teaching.* Cambridge, UK: Cambridge University Press.

Schmitt, N., & McCarthy, M. (Eds.). (1997). *Vocabulary: Description, acquisition, and pedagogy.* Cambridge, UK: Cambridge University Press.

Schrag, P. (2008, April 30). California's 1.6 million high-stakes English learners. *Sacramento Bee,* p. B7.

Schuemann, C.M. (2008). Myth 2: Teaching citation is someone else's job. In J. Reid (Ed.), *Writing myths: Applying second language research to classroom teaching* (pp. 18–40). Ann Arbor: University of Michigan Press.

Schwartz, G.G. (2004). Coming to terms: Generation 1.5 studens in mainstream composition. *The Reading Matrix, 4*(3), 40–57. Retrieved July 9, 2007, from www.readingmatrix.com/archives/archives_vol4_no3.html

Seymour, S., & Walsh, L. (2006). *Essentials of teaching academic reading.* Boston: Houghton Mifflin.

Sheen, Y. (2007). The effect of focused written corrective feedback and language aptitude on ESL learners' acquisition of articles. *TESOL Quarterly, 41,* 255–83.

Shin, H. B., & Bruno, R. (2003). *Language use and English-speaking ability: 2000.* Census 2000 Brief (October). www.census.gov/population/www/cen2000/briefs.html

Silva, T. (1990). Second language composition instruction: Developments, issues, and directions in ESL. In B. Kroll (Ed.), *Second language writing: Research insights for the classroom* (pp. 11–23). New York: Cambridge University Press.

————. (1993). Toward an understanding of the distinct nature of L2 writing: The ESL research and its implications. *TESOL Quarterly, 27,* 657–677.

————. (1994). An examination of writing program administrators' options for the placement of ESL students in first year writing classes. *Writing Program Administration, 18,* 37–43.

————. (1997). On the ethical treatment of ESL writers. *TESOL Quarterly, 31*(2), 359–363.

Silva, T., & Matsuda, P. K. (2002). Writing. In N. Schmitt (Ed.), *An introduction to applied linguistics* (pp. 251–266). London: Arnold.

Singhal, M. (2004). Academic writing and Generation 1.5: Pedagogical goals and instructional issues in the college composition classroom. *The Reading Matrix, 4*(3), 1–13. Retrieved July 9, 2007, from www.readingmatrix.com/archives/archives_vol4_no3.html

Slager, W. (1956). The foreign student and the immigrant: Their different problems as students of English. *Language Learning, 6,* 24–29.

Spack, R. (1988). Initiating ESL students into the academic discourse community: How far should we go? *TESOL Quarterly, 22*(1), 29–51.

————. (2004). The acquisition of academic literacy in a second language: A longitudinal case study, updated. In V. Zamel & R. Spack (Eds)., *Crossing the curriculum: Multilingual learners in college classrooms* (pp. 19–45). Mahwah, NJ: Erlbaum. (Reprinted from 1997 *Written Communication, 14,* 3–62)

————. (2006). *Guidelines* (3rd ed.). New York: Cambridge University Press.

Stegemoller, J. (2004). A comparison of an international student and an immigrant student: Experiences with second language writing. *The Reading Matrix 4*(3), 58–85. Retrieved July 9, 2007, from www.readingmatrix.com/archives/archives_vol4_no3.html

Swales, J. (1990). *Genre analysis: English in academic and research settings.* Cambridge, UK: Cambridge University Press.

Truscott, J. (1996). The case against grammar correction in L2 writing classes. *Language Learning, 46,* 327–369.

————. (2007). The effect of error correction on learners' ability to write accurately. *Journal of Second Language Writing, 16,* 255–272.

U.S. Department of Education, National Center for Educational Statistics (2003). *The condition of education 2003, NCES 2003-067.* Washington, D.C.: U.S. Government Printing Office.

Valdés, G. (2006). Bilingual minorities and language issues in writing: Toward professionwide responses to a new challenge. In P.K. Matsuda, M. Cox, J. Jordan, & C. Ortmeier-Hooper (Eds.), *Second-language writing in the composition classroom* (pp. 31–70). Boston: Bedford/St. Martin's. (Reprinted from 1992 *Written Communication, 9*(1), 85–136)

Weigle, S.C. (2002). *Writing assessment.* Cambridge, UK: Cambridge University Press.

Wolfe-Quintero, K., & Segade, G. (1999). University support for second-language writers across the curriculum. In L. Harklau, K. Losey, & M. Siegal (Eds.), *Generation 1.5 meets college composition: Issues in the teaching of writing to U.S.-educated learners of ESL* (pp. 191–209). Mahwah, NJ: Lawrence Erlbaum.

Wurr, A. (2004). English studies and Generation 1.5: Writing program administration at the crossroads. *The Reading Matrix, 4*(3), 14–23. Retrieved July 9, 2007, from www. readingmatrix.com/archives/archives_vol4_no3.html

Yi, Y. (2007). Engaging literacy: A biliterate student's composing practices beyond school. *Journal of Second Language Writing, 16*(1), 23–39.

Zamel, V. (1976). Teaching composition in the ESL classroom: What we can learn from research in the teaching of English. *TESOL Quarterly, 10*(1), 67–76.

———. (1982). Writing: The process of discovering meaning. *TESOL Quarterly, 16*(2), 195–209.

———. (1985). Responding to student writing. *TESOL Quarterly, 19*(1), 79–101.

Zhang, S. (1995). Reexamining the affective advantage of peer feedback in the ESL writing class. *Journal of Second Language Writing, 4*, 209–222.

———. (1999). Thoughts on some recent evidence concerning the affective advantage of peer feedback. *Journal of Second Language Writing, 8*, 321–326.

INDEX

Academic language, 25, 26–29, 106–113
  cognitive dimension of, 28
  complexity of, 33
  development of, 95–96
  dimensions of proficiency in, 26
  linguistic dimension of, 26–27
  sociocultural/psychological dimension, 29
  vocabulary knowledge in, 107–113
Academic listening and speaking, v
Academic literacy, iv–v, 25, 34
Academic L2 vocabulary, challenge of
  acquiring, 40
Academic oral skills of international
  students, 34–35
Academic reading, teaching strategies for
  word analysis in, 109–110
Academic Word List (AWL), 108, 109
Academic writing, 26
  lexical/syntactic variety in, 112
  raising awareness about lexical and
    syntactic variety, 112
  required skills, 39
Academic Writing Proficiency Examination
  (AWPE), 59
Acquisition/learning hypothesis, 32
Adamson, H. D., 38
Aebersold, J., 13, 27, 75, 80, 87, 91, 115, 126*n*1
Analytic essays, 87
Arndt, V., 120
Asenavage, K., 121
Assessment, 117, 137
  classroom, 97
Atkinson, D., 55, 61, 138

Bamford, J., 33, 40, 91, 92, 97, 114
Basic Interpersonal Communicative Skills
  (BICS), 8, 11, 18, 26, 33
Basic writing courses for monolingual
  English speakers, 55
Bates, L., 94, 126*n*1

Belcher, D., 35, 103, 104
Benson, B., 55, 61
Biber, D., 33
BICS/CALP distinction, 11, 29
Bilingualism, functional, 10–11, 19
Bilingualism Incipient, defined, 10
Bilinguals, circumstantial, 8, 10, 32
Bilinguals, elective, 8, 10, 12, 14, 77
Bilinguals, functional, 8, 15, 27
Bilinguals, incipient 8, 15, 16, 19
Birch, B. M., 27, 32, 36, 38, 40, 95, 109,
  110, 114, 115, 126*n*1
Bitchener, J., 5, 120, 126*n*3
Blanton, L. L., 19, 24*n*9, 54, 55, 56, 57, 61,
  65, 90, 126*n*1
Bosher, S., 5, 16, 19, 32, 33, 40
Braine, G., 53, 55, 61, 98, 121
Brinton, D., 5, 19, 20, 44, 55, 135, 147
Browning, G., 5, 19, 20, 44, 55, 135, 147
Bruce, S., 70, 123
Bruno, R., 3
Bunting, J., 27, 95, 112
Byrd, P., 27, 33, 80, 95, 108, 109–110, 112,
  126*n*1

California Pathways, 135
California State Standards for Language Arts
  Instruction, 32
Cameron, D., 120
Carro, G., 16, 18, 19, 20, 40, 55, 72*n*2
Casanave, C. P., 126*n*1
CATESOL Journal, 5, 133
CCCC Position Statement on Second
  Language Writing and Second
  Language Writers, 135
Chiang, Y-S., 20, 21, 54, 57, 72*n*1, 103
Ching, R., 5, 19, 20, 44, 55, 135, 147
Clark, Lisa Henry, 24*n*4
Classroom assessment and grading practices,
  course design and, 76, 97

163